D1522665

The Best of

DUNEDIN

Writers Group

2021

Jon Michael Miller, Editor

A special thank you to:

Joe Wisinski—Zoom coordination and proofreading,
Thomas McGann—proofreading,
John Whalen—proofreading,
Kevin Corrigan—cover photo of Dunedin area beach,
The hard-working members of the Promotions Committee:
     Patricia Pollack—computer graphics and more,
     Ellen Sollinger Walker—outreach and more,
     Margrit Goodhand—minutes, financial issues and more,
     Alexis Langsner—art work, outreach and more,
  also
All DWG members for their critiques, advice and support.

NOTICE

Several pieces contain violence and/or intense use of vernacular deemed essential for artistic verity.

This anthology is dedicated to

The healthcare workers and first-responders who have worked so hard for the nation

and

The United States military personnel who have sacrificed so nobly in Afghanistan.

"We tell stories in order to live." —Joan Didion

"A story has as many versions as it has readers."
—John Steinbeck

THIS IS JUST TO SAY

I have eaten
the plums
that were in
the icebox

and which
you were probably
Saving
for breakfast

Forgive me
they were delicious
so sweet
and so cold

—William Carlos Williams

EDITOR'S NOTE

These have been the world-changing months of the COVID19 Pandemic, from the solitude of which much of these writings have emerged. In our isolation, we kept our sprits strong by our Friday morning meetings online—and we evolved from a group to a family.

Entry into this volume was open to any of our members. The only requirements were the piece having been read to the group for critiques and readers' responses; also, rigorous proofreading. The entries were placed according to date of submission.

Dunedin Writers Group (DWG) has existed for approximately 20 years, founded by the late Mary T. Dresser whose writings can be found on Amazon and at the Dunedin Public Library, FL. The group looks forward to coming together in person at the library once again, and we greatly appreciate the support the staff has given us through the years.

Meeting each Friday, 9:30 a.m. until noon, we are a critique/reader-response group dedicated to making our writing as excellent as it can be. Writers on every level are welcome; all we ask is that you, like each of us, are seeking to improve your work. Many of us are local area residents, and others are snowbirds who keep in touch from points northward. Readers are welcome too, but be advised that you will soon be encouraged to put your fingers to the keyboard.

The Best of Dunedin Writing Group 2021 is our third annual anthology, and all three volumes are available in several local venues, in the Dunedin Public Library, and on Amazon. We encourage your reviews there, and/or comments at

mickymiller99@gmail.com.

CONTENTS

INTRODUCTION

Dave Easby

Every Friday for the past twenty years, a group of authors has met at the library in Dunedin, Florida, to share their works in progress and try to hone their craft. At first, you could count the number of members on the fingers of one hand but, as word of the quality of the writing and the feedback leaked out, membership soared. We moved from a staff boardroom barely larger than a phone booth to a meeting room the size of a primary school gymnasium. Like the tide at Clearwater Beach, membership ebbed and flowed over the years.

Florida has well earned its reputation as "God's Waiting Room" so, sadly, some people moved on to that great library in the sky. Others, well, they just moved on. But their chairs were quickly filled by new recruits anxious to learn from the group's critiques. And every winter, like the swallows to Capistrano, the Snowbirds flocked to Florida to take their places at the table.

But then 2020 happened and 'meet' became one of those four-letter words that was only spoken in hushed tones. Social distancing was no longer just something we did when Uncle Jack started moist-talking at Thanksgiving after one too many glasses of his dandelion wine. We collected masks like Imelda Marcos collected shoes and washed our hands so often that we uncovered those crib notes from a high school history test. And in Canada and many states, if you were busted for smoking dope at a family gathering, the illegal part was the family gathering.

Zoom allowed us to continue sharing our stories and fine-tuning our work. And while we all missed the camaraderie that only a face-to-face meeting provides, it allowed folks to join in from Canada and across the United States. In many ways, it helped bring us closer together.

As 2021 approached, a light appeared at the end of the tunnel that we all hoped was something other than an oncoming train. We listened intently as the talking heads on CNN debated the pros and cons of Pfizer versus Moderna versus AstraZeneca. This discussion, of course, in any other time would be carried out on the pages of *Lancet* and the *New England Journal of Medicine* among epidemiologists with unpronounceable names and an alphabet soup of credentials.

By early summer, we had lined up to get our shot, signed up for the workshops at Sweatpants Anonymous, and hurried off to get our clothes let out to disguise that extra pandemic poundage. We had booked a table at our favourite restaurant and asked our friends to join us, hoping we'd recognize the ones we had first met in the last year when they were masked up. The cardboard cutouts that filled the stands at TD Ballpark were replaced by living, breathing fans.

Sadly, however, the virus proved not quite ready to exit stage left. So, as fall approached, we retrieved the vaccination passports which we had stowed away in our safety deposit boxes, figuring they would become a great conversation piece one day. We rescued our masks from the sock drawer and kept mostly to home. But most of all, we prayed that that this fourth wave would last about as long as Mike Richard's tenure as the host of Jeopardy.

Experts keep telling us that we will experience a 'new' normal once the pandemic is finally over, and I certainly hope they're right. After all, when half the country thinks the other half is as nutty as a slice of Aunt Bea's fruitcake, and when our politicians struggle to even agree to disagree, the 'old' normal doesn't feel all that normal at all.

While we know you will be eager to finally get out and about once this is all *truly* behind us, if you feel a bizarre need to revisit the Covid years and self-isolate with a good book, we hope you will give this one a try. You will find stories from a wide range of genres in this anthology. There are short stories and excerpts from novels. Some have already been published and others are works in progress. If any of these pieces catch your fancy, there is information on the contributors' published works at the end of their contributions. We hope you will enjoy your new freedom when it does arrive – and *The Best of the Dunedin Writers Group 2021*.

◆

Dave is our chief Canadian tongue-in-cheek humorist. His later piece in this anthology, "Lack of Precision Air," is followed by a short biography and photo. He has kicked off each of our three annual anthologies with his wry and thoughtful opening comments.

DWG

JON MICHAEL MILLER

Gettysburg ... Again

Day One ... July 1, shortly after daybreak....

Patches of light mist hold off the early morning heat as a dented blue pickup moves westward on the Chambersburg Pike leaving the town of Gettysburg, Pennsylvania. The driver pulls over to a parking area beside a large statue of a soldier on horseback. The driver climbs out in work boots, blue jeans, white tee shirt, and blue cap. Late forties, he's wiry, strength in his wrists and forearms, lines of hard work on his face. He pours steaming coffee from a thermos into a tin cup, takes a sip, gazes at the green and light-brown fields, expanses of shaded broad-leafed woods, and scattered formations of breastworks and cannon.

A silver Cadillac speeds from the opposite direction, eastward toward the town, slows, and skids to a stop on the other side of the two-lane country road. Tall and dark-haired, in his early fifties, a man in a gray jogging suit gets out, stretches, yawns. With a pack of cigarettes and a lighter, he strides across the roadway, nods a greeting to the first arrival, looks up at the statue. He lights a cigarette, inhales deeply, lets smoke drift from his nostrils into the heavy air.

"I suppose you Yankees regard this man as quite a hero," he says with a Southern gentleman's accent.

"I don't follow the Yankees," the other answers. "I like the Phils."

"Ah, I see your wit is active quite early this mornin'."

"Anyway, how'd you know I'm from the North?"

The driver of the Cadillac points at the other's blue cap that says *Penn State*.

"Southerner, northerner," the truck owner says. "Ancient history, ain't it?"

Side by side, they take in the view.

"I am John Hampton. Lynchburg, Virginia."

"Bill O'Brien. Conshohocken. That's down near Philly."

"I am familiar with Conshohocken. My insurance firm has some clients up thataway."

They shake hands.

"Just caught a whiff of that coffee, Bill. Smells damned good."

"I was thinking the same about your smoke."

"Might I offer you one?"

"Thanks, "O'Brien says, "but I quit."

"Same here—supposedly. Caffeine, too. Doc's strict orders since my heart began actin' up. But some pleasures are just plain necessary." He takes a deep drag, stretches, surveys the scene. "Your heroic Colonel Buford blocked the road here with a small group of cavalry, held up our whole army until your infantry finally arrived. If not for Buford, you Yanks would have lost the high ground on Cemetery Hill that very first day—whole different outcome, whole different world. Amazin' how one little thing can lead to catastrophe."

"Catastrophe for one side," O'Brien says, "was success for the other. You sure know your history."

"Oh, I have read a little, watched some films, visited here several times. Family history as well."

"Family history?"

"Yessir, you are lookin' at a direct descendent of Major John Hampton, 19th Virginia. A representative from our family comes up here every now and then, a holy tradition. It is my turn to pay our respects. I wanted my boy to come along, but he says comin' up here is as excitin' as watchin' grass grow."

"Excuse me, was that the *19th Virginia* you said?"

"You sound surprised, Bill."

"Wait a minute." O'Brien goes to his truck, takes out a paper, studies it. "Pickett's Division, wasn't it?"

"You are exactly correct, sir. Marched right down the barrels of you bluebellies, the very pinpoint of the Great Charge. Our own Major Hampton lost his life in that valiant effort."

"This is damn weird."

"Why is that, Bill?"

"It just so happens I'm here because someone in my family died in the exact same attack. Sean Patrick O'Brien, only a private. The 19th Virginia fought against the 69th Pennsylvania, ain't that right?"

"By God, that *is* right, right on the button!"

Speechless, the two men look at each other, take deep breaths, re-state their names as if to make sure the coincidence is correct. It takes a few minutes for the amazing fluke of circumstance to sink in.

"How about," Hampton says, "in the light of this incredible stroke of providence, we join up for our little visit?"

"Well," O'Brien answers, "my daughter Sally had our plan to stay all three days. Booked the Holiday Inn—can't get our money back now—so I decided if I'm here, might as well do it up right. We were supposed to do this trip together, which I was looking forward to 'cause we don't spend as much time like we used to." He takes a sip of his coffee. "But she has to teach some classes for a prof that got sick. She studies history at Penn State and traced our family way back." He nods. "Ya see, I wanna get ahold of the events exactly like they happened. Sally wrote out this hour-by-hour schedule."

"All three days?" Hampton says. "I did that once. Goes slow as putty. My wife shopped the entire time, which is no small feat in this village. Today, I intend to stay just long enough to pay my respects. Besides insurance," he adds, handing O'Brien his business card, "I'm in real estate. Also, some farmin'—racehorses, Angus cattle and whatnot. You?"

"Electrician. I'm losing money, taking these weekdays off, but I promised Sally."

"Just wait until the family hears about our meetin' up like this!" Hampton says. "Our two forefathers, combattin' virtually face to face. What *are* the odds? Must be a billion to one."

"Maybe I *will* have that smoke," O'Brien says.

~

4

After Hampton takes a few snapshots, one of his new acquaintance, he moves on. The morning mist rising, O'Brien savors the ground of the initial fight his daughter made him read about. The battle started at this very spot with a division of Rebs marching from the west. O'Brien takes it in, feels it – Buford realizing he had to use his cavalry unit to hold them back. Across the road – McPherson's Ridge, the thick woods where Reynolds fell, the fence lines, clover meadows, wheat fields, the unfinished railroad cut that filled up with corpses of Confederates bushwhacked there.

He strolls, wanders the trails, reads the displays, climbs to the top of the observation tower, tries to sense the ghosts, to imbibe the reality of what happened, the eventual Southern domination of the field that first day, the Union troops fleeing helter-skelter through the town and up the ridge, now so serene in the distance.

Day Two, July 2 ...

A little after four in the afternoon, O'Brien struggles between huge rocks up the astounding boulder formation known as Devil's Den. Breathing hard, he reaches the Union battery at the top. The guns were overtaken by a gutsy unit of Texans. Although other visitors are milling about, O'Brien lingers to drink in the sense of the battle. Something stirs within him, something from the atmosphere of this now peaceful place, something he didn't feel from reading the book. He tries to understand the bravery of the fighters, wondering if *he* would have had the courage to stand up to the murderous clash. Staring across the rough terrain, he hears his name from behind – "Bill O'Brien!" It's John Hampton, out of breath from the ascent.

"I figured you would be over this way somewhere," he says, "*gettin' ahold of* the place as you phrased it. Finally spotted your truck. Whew, that's one heck of a climb."

"I thought you went home yesterday."

"I was on my way, but, you know, when I crossed the line into Maryland, I just *had* to turn around. I could *not* stop thinkin' about our runnin' into each other. So I stayed the night. Checked over at Culp's Hill this mornin', figured your daughter's schedule would take you over to those parts, but damned if I could find you."

"I was there, Spangler's Spring, in the woods."

"Oh-ho! You blueboys got your comeuppance at that pretty spot, a real bloodlettin'."

"I wasn't involved, if you realize it."

"A manner of speakin'. If it's not an intrusion, might I join up with you for a bit?"

"If you don't care about going real slow, like putty. I'm sticking to my program."

"I can take my leave if I get bored."

They scan the scene in silence.

"Longstreet did not want to fight here," Hampton says. "The whole thing was a dreadful miscalculation."

"He didn't like Lee's plan, so I guess he held off as long as he could."

"If you are suggestin' he purposely sabotaged his commander's orders, Bill, there you are mistaken. The reconnaissance was bad. Longstreet was forced to double-back and take another route so as not to be observed, wastin' precious time, not his fault. Then your madman General Sickles got in his way at the Peach Orchard. Longstreet could not have predicted you bluecoats pushin' forward so stupidly down from your line of defense."

"Hold your horses," says O'Brien. "The way I read it, Longstreet wanted to go all the way around, over that way." He points to the south of Big Round Top.

Hampton coughs a while, bent over, spits a wad of phlegm. "So, am I to take it you are contendin' Longstreet intentionally impaired Lee's plan?"

"That's the way the book tells it."

"No, sirree, he would never have done that."

"He didn't like Lee's strategy, even told him right to his face."

"Longstreet might have disagreed, but I must tell you, sir, he knew how to follow an order. And he won everything on this low ground that day, fought like the blazes, on Cemetery Ridge right over thataway. Almost broke your line."

"*Almost* only counts in horseshoes," O'Brien answers. "The book says the 69th Pennsylvania pushed back the men from Georgia over where you're pointing at, cut 'em to pieces. I read all about it."

"Who, may I ask, is the author of that book?"

"A man named Sears, like the store. Biggest book I ever read, but my Sally says it's the best."

"That Sears fella writes with a bias."

"Sally should know what's up. She's working on her Ph.D." O'Brien checks his schedule. "Time to head over to Little Round Top."

"Sorry about our little disagreement. Mind if I tag along?"

"All right, but no use arguing about spilt milk."

"Or," Hampton says, "more rightly put, spilt blood."

Back down the hill, they board their separate vehicles and drive to the boulder-strewn incline. Two-thirds of the way up, they park and meander along a forest path to the far-left flank of the Union line. Hampton takes out a tin of snuff, squeezes a pinch, and holds the container toward O'Brien, who declines.

"I better not light up out here," Hampton says, "with others wanderin' around. This mornin' an elderly lady thought she'd get cancer if she caught a sniff of my smoke."

"This general here was a real hero," O'Brien says.

"Chamberlain? He was hardly a general, and I don't know how much of a hero he was."

"He got the Medal of Honor, what more do you want?"

"Our effort on this end of the battle was weak, not well-manned, poorly coordinated. The troops were worn out from a long march that same day. Your precious Chamberlain gets far too much notoriety. Our boys lost it on their own."

"If what I read is right," Bill protests, "Chamberlain's men were all shot up, out of ammo, pledged to hold this place at all costs. When the bullets ran out, he ordered a bayonet charge down through them trees right down there."

"Our boys were plain tuckered out," Hampton insists.

They reach the line where Chamberlain's 20th Maine saved the Union flank. Had it failed, the Reb army would have swept along the ridge, rolling up the Union line, perhaps ending the war. O'Brien sits on a log. Hampton paces, his breathing audible. Other visitors stroll amid the foliage, whispering in reverence.

"Have you had enough?" Hampton says.

O'Brien checks his watch. "Time's not up yet. You go on ahead if you want to."

Hampton sighs, sits on the log, spits, takes another pinch. The two men stare down the slope into the verdant forest. Birds twitter in the green stillness. Now and then Hampton's wheezing interrupts the quiet.

Finally, O'Brien stands up, and they head toward Little Round Top's summit. From the height of their climb, the battle area of Sickles versus Longstreet is clear below.

"Can't you see," asks O'Brien, "why Lee was totally wrong to fight here? The only thing the Union guys had to do was roll down rocks."

"What you fail to comprehend," Hampton answers, bent over, heaving from the climb, "is that Lee was under the impression this hill was completely unoccupied."

"Longstreet shoulda told him the real deal."

"Hold on there, Bill. Lee had instructed him to attack, ordered him in no uncertain terms. It was already late in the day, and Longstreet had presented his alternate plan several times. What was he supposed to do? I'm sure if you'd been here, with your powerful hindsight, you would have won the victory for the South."

"No way I'da fought for the South."

"Jesus! I am speakin' hypothetically. You were extremely fortunate to have won the battle here. It could have been just as humiliatin' as all the other times you fought us—twice at Manassas, the Peninsula, Fredericksburg, especially Chancellorsville, even Sharpsburg, which you Yankees like to spin as a victory. You did not defeat us here. We defeated ourselves."

"That's right. Your great Robert E. Lee fell asleep at the wheel!"

"I would never disrespect his name by sayin' such a thing. Mistakes were made, there's no denying that, but they are mistakes exclusively in hindsight. Lee acted with the best information he had. If you recall your precious book, which is clearly prejudiced, Lee's whole cavalry, his eyes and ears, were missin' the entire week."

"Yeah, Jeb Stuart, roaming around killing and robbing people for his own fun."

"Sir, you are beginning to grate on my nerves."

"Look, I came here to get the feeling of this place, not to listen to you defend Robert E. Lee's screw-ups."

I can see my presence has become an intrusion, sir. So, if you do not mind, I shall be on my way."

~

Alone, O'Brien climbs to the very top boulder. He's agitated from the conversation with Hampton, but after a while, the sun drifting farther west, he settles down. By this time during the conflict, the Rebels had withdrawn, the fields, woods and rocky ravines thick with the dead and wounded, smoke hovering like fog, screams of pain. It became known as the Slaughter Pen. O'Brien closes his eyes, tries to capture it. Hampton was right about small events leading to big consequences. If the Southern leaders had made wiser decisions, how different the world would be today—two countries instead of one!

Bill O'Brien can't remember ever having been moved in quite this way. He wants to … pray. He isn't a man of faith, never offers grace at the family get-togethers, but nothing less than, yes, *prayer,* seems appropriate. Tears come to his eyes. Silently, he recites … *Our Father, who art in heaven, hallowed be Thy name….*"

Day Three, July 3 …

O'Brien drives along the Southern line on Seminary Ridge. He stops at Lee's memorial and wanders out into the field where the famed general observed the fatal charge. O'Brien stands where Lee stood. He imagines being a Southern soldier ordered to march across those fields and climb over those fences toward where the Union men waited in an impregnable position, cannon fire raining down upon the marching Rebs. O'Brien is stunned that those soldiers did not rise up in mutiny against their generals. Again, he ponders his own courage. He can't help but feel compassion for what happened to all those Southerners that day.

After a while, he drives over to the Union line on Cemetery Ridge, parks at the southern end, and begins his hike, pausing among other visitors to inspect each marker and monument, North and South. Of the memorials, Pennsylvania's is the largest, all the names of the commonwealth's dead engraved on granite walls.

Among the mostly other Irish names of the 69th, O'Brien locates his distant relative's, Sean P. O'Brien. The day is hot, heavy. O'Brien has trouble keeping tears back. Not a man to cry, he doesn't like the feeling. But something profound has opened to him, something he hadn't realized about … well, about life itself. The wonder of the feeling is too big, too deep, to give it a name.

Through blurred vision he can see Lee's monument almost two miles across the field. He notices the barn where Pickett's troops were forced to divide before continuing their march to devastation.

When O'Brien reaches the low stone wall where the Pennsylvanians rebuffed the Georgians the day before, he sits on the edge and gazes over the wide expanse toward the trees. He imagines what it was like the third day, the Confederate artillery gleaming in the distance, standing ready along a mile-and-a-half line, the eerie silence waiting for what would happen. Then he pictures the cannonade, the shells whining in, exploding, creating smoke, death, chaos, horses screaming, men groaning, for over an hour before the Rebel troops emerged from the faraway woods and formed their marching positions.

He strolls along the wall, envisioning the awe and fear the Northern soldiers must have felt. He places himself in Private Sean O'Brien's boots, kneeling low, musket aimed, waiting. According to the book, beside him probably lay three or four loaded rifles collected from yesterday's dead and wounded. The brigade consisted of veterans all, Hancock's corps, in the center of the long blue line, the exact point of Lee's attack, led by, yes, the 19th Virginia.

He moves to the copse of trees, the focal point of Lee's artillery barrage. Just past the grove, the stone wall takes a right turn, known as the Angle, the one point actually reached by the assault. There, he stops, closes his eyes, feels the moment.

By now the Union howitzers are firing back into the mass of humanity marching toward him, mowing the enemy down without mercy. General Lee believed God would support his cause against the odds. How wrong he was! O'Brien senses the anticipation of the men, smells the musket fumes, feels the trembling of earth under his body. The Southern troops are here now, bayonets, hand to hand.

"Bill!" Hampton's voice.

O'Brien turns. Hampton strides toward him. O'Brien almost bolts, then holds his ground.

"I knew you would be in this location about now," Hampton says, "followin' your precious schedule. Something you said yesterday has been eatin' at my craw all night. You stated you would never have fought for the South. That's a crazy thing to say. Had you lived in the South, you would most surely have understood something you're grossly ignorant about."

"Why didn't you go back to Virginia, Hampton?"

"It gets my goat that even now you Yankees think you are quite superior, quite smug, when you are actually quite blindly uninformed." His face is flushed with anger.

"I certainly wouldn't have fought for slavery."

"This war was not about slavery! What will it take to get that point through your thick Yankee skulls?"

"What's that? Not about slavery? Are you nuts?"

"Our fight was about the freedom that our nation was founded upon, a freedom that was betrayed by you people, in the name of *Union*. It was about not being ruled by a damnable tyrant. America was not meant to have a king."

"Tyrant? King? Do you mean Abraham Lincoln?"

"He wanted to be Caesar. Even your beloved General Grant acknowledged the dedication we showed to our cause."

"Didn't Grant say you were fighting for the *worst cause possible*? That was slavery."

"You twist his words, sir. Like you twist everything. We know Grant's respect for our ideals from readin' his extremely respectful terms of surrender. Without Lincoln's quest for absolute power, this war would never have occurred." Hampton's breathing is heavy, his eyes wild.

"What about your slaves?" O'Brien asks. "Where would they be in your racist world? You'd probably have a bunch of them right now in your own mansion down there in Lynchburg, cutting your grass and cooking your fucking grits."

Hampton lunges, grabs O'Brien by the throat. O'Brien drops to his knees, slips away, tackles Hampton around the ankles. They struggle, wrangle. The fighting is intense. Soon onlookers notice. The two men grapple, grunt, sweat, roll on the wet grass and mud. Neither relents. O'Brien pounds Hampton in the gut; Hampton punches O'Brien on the chin, smashes O'Brien's head back against the rock wall. Hampton takes advantage, pounds O'Brien's skull against the rocks. Stunned, neck bursting blood, O'Brien shoves violently back. Hampton rolls away, groans, grasps his left arm. Both men are bloody, their clothes soiled and ripped. O'Brien tries to remain conscious, struggles to get to his knees, fails, topples onto Hampton. He tries to cry out but cannot. Hampton writhes beneath him, gasps. Exhausted, O'Brien holds his own neck, lies still, cannot move. He gives up. Sunlight blurs, dulls. All goes dark. He can't see, hear. Then … nothing.

A crowd gathers around the two men who lie tangled together. As if astounded, Hampton gazes upward. When Park rangers arrive, he still struggles, knees twitching. A female officer tugs O'Brien off, checks his gaping neck wound, takes his pulse.

"My God!" she cries. "This man is dead! Must have lost half his blood!"

Two other rangers check Hampton, whose eyes are wide with panic. "This one seems … dam it—his heart!"

Hampton's groans grow fainter. His eyes close. An officer pushes on his chest, keeps working but finally gives up the effort. It's no use. He turns to the many witnesses, shouts, "What the hell happened here! What is this all about?"

Jon Michael Miller earned three degrees in English from Penn State. A native of Lancaster County PA, he has taught at Penn State, Ohio State, and St. Pete College. His novel, *Murder and Mayhem at Tropic Gardens,* earned 5 stars from Readers' Favorite. His historical novel about Kent State has inspired accolades from those who were there during those dreadful days of May 1970. Living in northwest St. Pete with his wife Yukika, Mike writes, edits, and facilitates independent publishing.

Buy these books (and others) at amazon.com/author/jonmichaelmiller

DWG

BARBARA SCHREFER

Doing Your Bit in 1942

Everyone wondered why she'd married him, but nobody said anything. It wasn't done to discuss things like that; seemed rude. But she was lovely, my Aunt Cathy, with red gold curls and white skin, and just a few freckles on her nose. She was the star of the show, the spoiled only child, the magnet. In front of her I always stumbled and gawked, twelve years old, terrified of speaking. "And what have you been doing with yourself, Barbara?" she would ask, and I wouldn't be able to think of anything to say, in the end turning away in confusion. What had I been doing with myself? Nothing really, except going to school. What did they expect me to say? I'd chew the end of my braid, turn to my father for help, but he'd just shake his head.

Now, my Uncle Bill was a go-getter, a thin man a head shorter than Cathy. He was no oil painting. My father said he looked like a skinned rabbit, didn't know why Cathy married him. You see, my father didn't like Uncle Bill, but perhaps that was because Bill was a Catholic, a wicked, sinful, idolatrous papist – I didn't know. It was confusing, the grown-up world.

What I did know was that Bill loved Cathy. He adored, idolized and treasured her. My mother told me he prayed every night he wouldn't get called up and paid for masses to be said to get out of being in the army, because he couldn't have borne it if he'd have had to leave her. Actually, it was flat feet that got him out of it, that and being so small. So, he worked himself to death instead selling red petrol, and had some great fiddle with the coupons, my dad said, and made a packet of money on the black market.

After a few months he bought a lovely house for Cathy, overlooking the sea. Cathy didn't have to lift her little finger and had a woman in to "do" for her. Bill did all the cooking and shopping, even after a hard day's work, and she always said to everyone, "He's the best little husband anyone could have." The only problem for Uncle Bill, so my mother said, was that he was in torment every day because he was jealous of Cathy, jealous of any man looking at her, jealous of the postman, the milkman, the dustbin man, the bus conductor, and the priest who heard her confession. When she went to church, he would be outside the confessional straining his ears to find out what she was saying, darting back to his pew when she came out.

Cathy's main love was the piano, and she was in the Palm Court Orchestra at the Winter Gardens on the weekends. Bill couldn't get her to give it up and would stand by the grand piano, part of an adoring group of men, he much smaller than the rest of them, looking silly, white-faced with exhaustion after his week's work.

The war dragged on and we all had to do our bit, like they said on the wireless. My dad was called up and my mother went into a factory and riveted airplanes, making sure she did a good job so those lovely young men wouldn't come crashing down and lose their lives. I had to carry a gas mask all the time in a brown cardboard case that got soggy when it rained. We spent some nights in the Anderson shelter, but it didn't bother me much because my mum was there and so everything was all right.

We wondered, sometimes, what was going on at Uncle Bill's. Had he managed to pull strings and get Cathy out of doing her bit? We didn't have a car or telephone, and the trains were taken up by soldiers, so the only way you could find out anything was by letter, and you couldn't write down something like that, couldn't say, "How are you, Cathy, and have you been doing your bit, or has Bill got you out of it?"

Quite a long time went by and then, one day, when I got home from school, who should I see in the front parlor, talking to my mother, but Uncle Bill. I'd caught sight of him through the window and gone running up to wave at him, but when I saw he was crying and his nose was bright red, and his face all screwed up I drew back. After that I took a peep and saw that his shoulders were shaking, his hands twisting his big white hanky into a rope. My mother caught my eye and made a big shooing motion with her arms, like I was a goose, and I slunk round the back and into the kitchen.

They seemed to be in there for hours. I was starving hungry but daren't get anything to eat, my mother had our rations worked out down to the last crumb and I would have caught it good and proper if I'd taken anything.

Finally, I heard some shuffling and more sobbing, and my mother's voice syrupy and comforting. "There, there,

Bill, don't take on so, it'll all blow over, it's the war, you know," and then the front door shutting quietly.

"Oh, what a to-do this is," she said, coming into the kitchen, wringing her hands on her apron. "That poor fellow's just off his head."

"What's up, Mum" I asked.

"None of your business," she said. "You're too young to understand this lot, but I'll tell you something, that Cathy never was any good for him, she thinks because she plays the piano she's better than the rest of us. She doesn't even put up her raspberries and he's grown them for her special and all." She glared at me as though it was my fault, then cut me a piece of bread, spread it with margarine, thought for a moment, scraped off half the margarine, and smeared it on another piece.

Shortly after that we got a card in the post. It said a son had been born to Cathy and Bill, eight pounds ten ounces. My mother didn't look very pleased, though, or knit anything and send it, and I thought it a bit queer, but daren't say anything.

When my dad came home on leave, I knew the story would come out. I knew my mother would tell him what had gone on after I had gone to bed, so I wrapped myself in a blanket, crept halfway down the stairs to the exact spot where I knew I could hear but not be seen, if the door opened, and waited.

After a while, my father said, "What's going on with your Bill, then? How did he manage to get a bun in Cathy's oven? He must have had the Archangel Gabriel come down and give him a lift. I didn't think he had it in him, to tell you the truth."

"Don't be like that, George," said my mother. "That poor fellow has been through the torments of hell itself. It's his own fault for marrying someone with red hair. I knew no good would come of it."

"What I don't understand," said my father, "is what he sold that lovely big house for, I mean having a baby and all you'd think they'd be needing more room, not less. I can't believe it's because they're short of money. He'll always have a bob or two, that one, and there's nothing gone wrong with the black market as far as I can see."

"Oh, I have a proper tale to tell you, George. There's a lot you don't know. Poke the fire and I'll make a cup of tea, then I'll get on with the story."

I had to sit, then, on the freezing stairs, listening to the settling coals, the rattling cups and saucers and the hissing of boiling water being poured into the tea pot.

"Well, this is what happened," said my mother, finally. "About six months ago I'd just got back from the shops when I saw William getting off the bus at the corner. Seven hours it'd taken him to get here from Morecambe, you know what busses are like, these days."

"Get on with it," said my dad.

"Well, it turns out that the War Office sent them a letter saying that Cathy had to do something – something apart from playing the piano and looking like Rita Hayworth, once she'd had her hair done, that is. Seems Cathy had a choice. She could work in a factory like me – can you imagine it, Miss High and Mighty getting them long red nails round a riveting gun, or she could take in evacuees, or they could have a soldier billeted on them. They thought about the evacuees, but you never know what you're getting, you know. Some of them children have nits in their hair, and sore ears, and Mrs. Dryden got two who'd never used a knife and fork before, at least that's what she said, and she couldn't get them clean – they had tides round their necks you couldn't scrub off – and they had infections, too."

"What's that got to do with Cathy?"

"I'm telling you. What they finally decided was to have a soldier; he would be out most of the time and he could have his own room and keep to himself."

"Oh aye, so what went wrong?"

"What went wrong? I'll tell you what went wrong. First off, he looked like Tyrone Power, that's what went wrong. On top of that he's an officer with a posh voice like he went to public school, with lovely manners and our Bill only came up to his chest, and this officer – Brian something his name was – took one look at Cathy and they clicked. He didn't seem to go out at all, even spent his leave at Bill's house. That's when our Bill twigged something was going on."

"He was always the jealous kind, your Bill. What did he do about it?"

"What could he do? He suffered torments, that's what he did. This fellow Brian started cooking for her and bringing wine home, and you know Bill can't drink that fancy foreign stuff, it upsets his stomach something terrible. And this Brian and Cathy always had their heads together, laughing, and she starts wearing some French sounding scent, and painting her toenails red, and I don't know what else. Our Bill used to go running home at all times, moidered to death about what was going on, and frightened to death of finding out. Anyhow, you know what happened next, don't you?"

"No, what did happen?"

"You great lummox, what do you think? She tells Bill she's expecting, that's what. And he turns into a mad man, throwing pots around, and pans, and even some of his Crown Derby china – and you know how much that costs, not that you can get it anymore with the war and all."

"He threw his Crown Derby around?"

"Yes, that's how upset he was, and she's crying, and he's crying, and the soldier, what does he do, he asks to be billeted somewhere else – unfavorable conditions – that's what he said. Anyway, after a lot of crying and moaning, Bill said he'd forgive her and bring up the child."

"How did he know it wasn't his?"

"How do you think he knew it wasn't his, you stupid fool."

"Oh aye, I see what you mean," said my dad, after a minute.

"Well, the next news is the War Office said they had to take in another soldier because they had all that room. But Bill wasn't having any – you know how wily he can be- so he sold that lovely house and now they are living in a row house in a back street with an outside lavatory and two miserable little bedrooms, not even a bathroom. No room for any soldiers in there. Those houses should have been condemned, that's what I say.

"But do you know what I think, George," she continued, "I think that's how Bill is punishing her. I don't think they'll ever leave that back street, not ever, and she'll be living there 'til she dies, and Bill doesn't care – he'll keep her a prisoner in that little house forever and a day."

"I reckon you're right," my father said, with a sigh.

At this point I carefully, on hands and knees, got to the top of the stairs, pulled my frozen body into bed, lying shivering under the sheets, thinking about Aunt Cathy. It reminded me of a story I'd heard once, about a man walling up his wife in a castle while she was alive because she'd been unfaithful to him and leaving her there to die.

My mother was right, they never did leave the little house. Many of the surrounding back streets were torn down for slum clearance, but for some reason that street remained standing.

The boy grew into a big, tall, excessively handsome young man, who looked remarkably like Tyrone Power. It's funny, isn't it, people whispered, that a runty little fellow like Bill has such a big, fine lad for a son.

As her son grew, Cathy seemed to shrink. The red hair faded, the piano was sold. I once heard her say, in a sad moment, "It was the war, you know, the terrible war. That was the cause of it all. It wouldn't have happened if I hadn't had to do my bit."

Barbara Schrefer was born in Lancashire, England in the 1930s and has memories of a World War II childhood. In her twenties she lived in London and Paris. In the early sixties she came to America, and has lived in San Francisco, New York, and now in Clearwater. For a chapter of her novel *Marlene,* she received the Maryland State Arts Council Individual Artist Award in Fiction and won first prize in the Florida State Writing Competition, novel category. Professor Les Standiford, one of the judges for the competition, made these remarks: "This is lovely, sensitive writing about a young working-class woman struggling to establish an identity in England of the 1950s. The sense of place, the humor, the deft handling of characterization, the knowledge of what it means to be human, the ongoing development of story and conflict, all suggest this book will soon find a place on a good publisher's list. Absolutely first rate, mature work. I was sorry to have to leave off reading."

Buy Barbara's book on Amazon Books.

DⓌG

JOE WISINSKI

But We Have Good Video
A Novella about Television News

Chapter One

Friday, 5:15 p.m.

WERI TV news assignment manager Dave Wilson closed his front door and tossed his jacket on the couch. The pleasant aroma of roast beef reached him as he called out "Hi, sweetie!" and walked to the kitchen. His girlfriend, Marti, already home from her job, was setting the table. Putting his arms around her, he brushed her blond hair aside and kissed the back of her neck. He felt her quiver as he ran his hands up and down her body. She turned around, her lips met his, and he savored the familiar sweetness of her mouth.

For a minute the newsroom noise that still lingered in Dave's head ceased. The phones that never stopped ringing. The non-stop clatter of keyboards. The never-ending questions from his boss and colleagues. The abusive complaints from viewers. All disappeared and he heard nothing except Marti's heavy breathing.

Marti's mouth roamed along Dave's neck and as she nibbled on his ear he stopped thinking about the constant pressure to develop new story ideas. About the details that the newsman in him wanted to see in TV news stories, but which they never included.

Her lips returned to his and her tongue explored his mouth. When their kiss ended Dave's voice turned husky. "Keep that up and we won't be eating dinner."

A smile slowly spread across her face, creating dimples under her blue eyes. "You know, that roast could slow cook for another hour."

His eyes danced. "I like how you're thinking." He kissed her again and pushed his hand into the small of her back. Her body pressed into his and a spoon clattered on the floor as it slipped from her fingers.

With their lips locked they stumbled clumsily toward the bedroom, tearing at their clothes like a parody of a movie scene. Dave's tie landed on the hall floor, followed a moment later by Marti's blouse.

They fell on the bed together, locked in passionate embrace, as Dave reached around her to unfasten her bra. He had just pulled it away when he heard a familiar *ring-ring*. His hand instinctively shot into his pocket and pulled the phone out. The caller ID read "Angela Holmes." The TV station's news director. His boss. Dave grunted. "No way." His finger reached for the "decline" button, but he glanced at Marti. The look on her face said, "go ahead."

"This can't be important," Dave assured her. "I'll just tell Angela whatever she needs to know and get back to. . ."

He hit "answer."

Angela's voice came through crisply and without a word of introduction or apology. "We need you to come back in."

Dave's chest tightened and he paused before replying. "Why? What happened?"

"A plane made a hard landing at the Erie airport."

"What do you mean 'a hard landing?' Did someone get killed?"

"No."

"Injured?"

"Not as far as we know."

"Did the plane slide off the end of the runway?"

"No. It's sitting on the tarmac now. Everyone evacuated safely on the emergency slide."

"Then what do you need me for?"

Angela's voice took on a matter-of-fact tone. "Here's what happened. A guy was driving by on Asbury Road. He saw the plane flying crazily as it approached the runway. Bouncing up and down and twisting from side to side. He grabbed his phone and got video of the whole thing—the last few moments of the flight, the hard landing, people going down the slide, everything."

"So?"

"It's great video and we're the only station that has it. So it's a big story."

With his free hand Dave soundlessly slapped his forehead. "Even though no one's hurt and the situation is over." He thought about his nightside colleague. "What about Ron? Isn't he making calls?"

A note of irritation crept in as Angela answered. "Of course. But he needs help. We want to keep running the video, but we need to update the voiceover. That's why you have to come in. We need more information."

Dave thought about arguing that they didn't have to keep running the video. It wasn't an ongoing story. He said nothing, but made no attempt to conceal a sigh.

Angela's voice hardened. "It's the news business, Dave. You know that. You work when we need you."

News business, baloney, he thought. *TV news is infotainment at best.*

He sighed again. "I'll be there in 15 minutes." He punched the "end" button and shoved the phone back in his pocket. "I have to go back to work."

"Why? What's going on?"

"Nothing." He scowled. "But we have good video."

Marti sat up and grabbed her blouse. She covered herself and said, "Not again. I thought you said you were going to talk to Angela about not doing stories only because the video is compelling."

"I tried." Dave involuntarily thought back to the conversation in Angela's office. He remembered her fingers drumming on her desk. He knew what that meant . . . whenever Angela drummed her fingers it meant her patience was running out and he was about to be taken to the principal's office.

"I got about three sentences in before she stopped me. 'It's TV,' is all she said."

"Can't we at least eat dinner together?"

"I'm sorry. No." He touched her cheek and kissed her on the forehead. "I have to take a rain check, both on dinner and on . . ."

~

As he drove back to the station Dave cranked an oldies station up loud, trying to forget what he left at home. He mentally composed the questions he would ask sources. *Where did the flight originate? How many were on board? How old is the plane? What experience did the flight crew have with that aircraft?* A dozen more questions floated through his mind.

But even as he thought of the questions, he knew that few details would make air. As Angela said, they only wanted more facts so they could continue running the "great video." He comforted himself with the knowledge that at least their web editor would use whatever details he dug up.

Dave punched a radio button to change stations as a commercial came on. Before returning his hand to the wheel he clenched it into a fist. *Why did I leave print news? I thought TV news would be glamorous. Some glamor, dragging myself back to work at 6:30 on a Friday night. And some excuse for news. All we're doing is trying to get eyeballs on our video. We might as well be YouTube.*

Chapter Two

Friday, 5:45 p.m.

As Dave entered the TV station he heard the banging of a hammer and the roar of a power saw. Trailing down the hall he stepped around construction material and equipment, but not before stubbing a toe on a box marked "electric cable." *What's all this stuff doing here?* Then he remembered—

31

work on an updated news set started that evening. He grunted. *Right. Like a cooler-looking set will attract more viewers.*

Even before he reached the newsroom he took in the pungent odor of tuna fish. *Ron must be eating dinner at his desk. Gag. Even my cat would hate that smell.* As he approached their cubicle Ron finished a phone call and turned to him. "What are you doing here?"

Dave rolled his eyes. "Angela called me. She told me to come back and help you with calls about the plane incident."

"I don't need any help. I've already talked to pretty much everyone. The airport authority. Millcreek Police. I left messages with the airline, but no one's called back."

Dave sat down and logged on to his computer. "Who did you assign the story to?"

"Sarah and Ben. I sent them to the airport."

"Who did they talk to?"

"A couple of people. Sarah got the guy who shot the video and also one of the passengers. They tried talking to airport employees, but no one inside the airport had seen the landing or knew anything."

"So between you and Sarah you've done everything we can for now, right?

Ron spread his arms out. "Yes, we're good to go."

"Then what am I doing here?"

"Don't ask me." Ron turned back to his sandwich. "There's nothing more you can do."

Dave thought about how he left Marti to return to the station. *Well, I can't just go home again. Angela may check up on me. I'll find something to do.* He opened his email and read numerous messages about the plane. One from Angela read, "Jump all over this story!" Dave grunted. *While we're at it let's jump all over "sun rose this morning."*

He looked out over the newsroom. Beside Ron, only a producer, the web editor, and their news anchor were working. Their sports reporter was out covering a basketball game. Everyone else was gone for the weekend, even their meteorologist, who had recorded his forecast before leaving. Seven TVs hung from a wall, one for each or the local channels, along with three from national news stations. One TV, the one tuned into WERI, had the sound turned up; all the rest were muted. The only other sound came from the hallway, where the workmen continued their construction. Even the phones were mostly quiet. *Friday night and I'm in a near-empty newsroom. What was that again about the glamor of TV news?*

Jazzy music announcing the start of the 6 o'clock news interrupted his musing. "While I'm here I might as well do the comps for you," he said to Ron, referring to the practice of watching their competitors' broadcasts.

"Thanks," Ron mumbled as he chewed his sandwich.

As Dave flipped back and forth between the three other stations, he saw none had broadcast any information that WERI didn't have. One of them, WLAK, hadn't even led with the story. They started with the weather; their meteorologist said a big snowstorm would arrive Sunday morning.

Dave also watched his station's coverage of the landing. News anchor Jeff Nelson led off the broadcast.

"An incoming flight made a hard landing at the Erie airport late this afternoon. WERI has exclusive video of this incident. Our Sarah Sanchez is live on scene with the story."

With the January temperature standing at 30 degrees Sarah stood inside the airport terminal. She raised a microphone to her mouth. "Jeff, we're told the flight was inbound from Philadelphia. High winds buffeted the plane as it approached. One of our viewers filmed the landing. He said he'd never seen a plane land like that before."

The story switched to the man who had provided WERI with the video. "I was just driving by and I saw this plane weaving in the air. Then it landed—boom—and the emergency slide opened. People started leaping out."

The story continued with Sarah's voiceover as the man's video played. "Passengers said the flight was about two-thirds full."

The video showed the aircraft hit the runway, bounce once, then slowly come to a stop. "Despite what you see here," Sarah said, "we're told that no one was injured."

The screen changed to a middle-aged man and woman as Sarah said, "Passenger Robert Fischer and his wife Kathy were on the flight."

"It was a little bumpy on the way in," Robert Fischer said. "I've seen worse." Kathy Fischer added, "I don't see why we had to jump on the slide."

Sarah came back on screen with her reporter tag. "We reached out to the airline for comment. They haven't returned our calls. On scene at the airport, I'm Sarah Sanchez, WERI news."

The screen returned to Jeff in the studio. "We will of course continue to investigate this story. We'll keep you updated as we learn more. Turning to the weather, expect a big change over the weekend."

Dave hit the mute button as the broadcast switched to their meteorologist. "I don't believe this," he said to Ron. "Even the passengers say it wasn't a big deal." He leaned back in his chair, put his hands behind his head, and paused before asking his colleague, "So, what do you think about all this?"

Ron didn't answer for a moment as he tore open a package of cookies. "Well, it really isn't much of a story." He reached for a ringing phone. "But it is pretty cool video."

Chapter 3

Friday, 6:45 p.m.

As Dave expected, Angela called the newsroom to check on the story's progress. Ron picked up the call and turned to his colleague. "It's Angela. For you."

He glanced at the time. *Good. After I talk to her I'll go home. Back to Marti.*

"I saw the 6 o'clock story," Angela said. "It wasn't any different than our 5 o'clock broadcast."

"That's right. We had no updated information."

"Why not? What about the airport? Did you call the spokesperson?"

"Yes. We left a message on her cell. She never called back."

"Then call her again. What about her home number? Don't you have that?"

"Well, maybe. Or I suppose we could find it. But—"

Angela cut him off. "Then call her at home. Or send Sarah to get her on camera."

Dave took a deep breath and struggled to keep his patience, "Look, maybe if we bug her enough we'll get a comment. But next week or next month we're going to contact her on a different story. And you know she's going to think about tonight and say, 'It's those so-and-sos from WERI calling again.'"

Angela said nothing for a moment. *Surely she got my point.*

But she resumed. "This is a big story. And we're the only station with video. We need an updated story at 11."

"But what about the snowstorm?" Dave asked. You know we're supposed to get maybe a foot on Sunday."

"I know. But tonight we have video of an airplane, not a snowstorm."

Dave didn't quit. "And there was that city council meeting this morning. They made a big decision about—

"And what video do we have from that meeting, Dave?"

He tried once more. "You know, I watched the airplane video and the quality isn't all that great. I don't see—"

Angela cut him off again. "I don't agree. I think it's good video and I want it to keep running." She said nothing for a moment, but Dave heard the drumming of her fingers.

He sighed. "All right. I'll do what I can." But even as he spoke he told himself *No way I'm calling the spokesperson at home. And I'm sure not sending Sarah to her house.* Another plan began formulating. He hung up and walked over to Gina, the evening newscast's producer.

Gina's eyes stayed glued on her computer screen as Dave approached. "I just talked to Angela," he said. "She wants the airplane story updated for 11."

"What new information do we have?"

"That's just it. Nothing. But I have an idea."

Gina stopped typing and turned to him. "What are you thinking?"

"Why don't we do this . . . let's edit the guy's video and switch the order. First, we'll show passengers jumping on the emergency slide. Then the plane's approach. And finally the landing itself. Then it won't look like the same story we showed at 5 and 6."

She pursed her lips. "That might work."

Dave nodded. "Sarah's voiceover will change, obviously. She can first say something like 'passengers were forced to jump on a plane's emergency slide at the airport this afternoon.' Then when we show the approach she'll say 'the incident happened after strong winds hit the plane.'"

Gina clicked on the 11 p.m. lineup and began typing. "And then when we show the plane hitting the runway Sarah will say 'those high winds caused a hard landing.'"

"Right." He rubbed his hands together. "So we have all the same information, but in a different order and with new VO."

"I like the idea," Gina said. She stopped typing and turned to him. "But it's not going to fool Angela, you know."

"I know. But viewers will think we updated the story. That's all Angela cares about—making it at least look like we're broadcasting new information."

Gina gave him a thumbs up and thought for a moment. "You know the other thing we can do? Let's put up a 'breaking news' banner."

"Good idea." Dave remembered a graphic he'd once seen on CNN—"Breaking news: Titanic sunk 102 years ago tonight." *At least our "breaking news" is more recent than that.*

But as he headed back to his desk his head drooped. *Really? Is this what our newscasts have become? Just broadcasting stories that are less ridiculous than 102-year-old news?* His spirits plunged further when he realized *and that's the level I'm sinking to.*

When he reached his desk Dave shut down his computer and said to Ron, "Okay. I'm heading home. Again." He grabbed his coat and started to leave, but turned back. "Did you hear what Gina and I decided on for 11?"

Ron nodded. "That works."

"Right. But if the airport spokesperson calls back or you get any new information do me a favor—call and let me know." Ron nodded again. "Sure. Enjoy your weekend."

"I will." He remembered leaving Marti in the bedroom. *You bet I will.*

On the way home, Dave pounded the steering wheel as he recalled the last hour. *What did I accomplish? I pretty much gave my boss a lecture and suggested Gina do something she probably would have done anyway. What a waste. But at least . . .* His thoughts dissolved to a vision of Marti waiting for him.

When he walked in Marti was sitting on the couch with a bowl of popcorn. He expected her to be wearing pajamas or a nightie, but she wore ragged jeans and a t-shirt. A strap peeking out showed him she'd put her bra back on. Her hair was in a bun. "Hello," she said, with her mouth full. "How did it go?"

"All right. As I said, there was no reason to go back. Ron and Gina had everything under control." He plopped down next to her. "Angela got on my case for not calling the airport spokesperson back. I essentially told her I wasn't going to do that. Then Gina and I manipulated the video a bit to make it look like updated news."

He stared at the ceiling. "What a waste TV news is. Video. Video. Video. That's all they want. They don't care how big the story is, they only want to know 'what are the visuals?'"

Dave started to go on, but Marti yawned and began to thumb through a magazine. He kissed her cheek and began to move toward her mouth, but she grabbed another handful of popcorn and shoved it in. He tried to nuzzle her neck, but its tantalizing softness moved away as she grabbed a drink.

He settled back on the couch and put his hand on her knee, then slowly moved up her leg. "So, ready to continue where we left off?"

Marti finished her snack and got up. She walked toward the kitchen with the empty bowl. "Not now. I'm getting tired. Besides, I want to watch 'Jeopardy.'"

He watched as she rinsed the bowl and put it in the dishwasher. She began rummaging through cupboards and drawers as he waited for her to return. "What are you doing?"

"Nothing."

Marti left the kitchen and headed to their bathroom. Moments later Dave heard the sound of brushing teeth. She returned just in time for *"Jeopardy,"* grabbed the remote, and sank into her seat at the other end of the couch.

Dave knew better than to talk while her show was on, but after the players answered "Final Jeopardy" he turned to Marti. "Okay. Tell me. What's going on?"

"What do you mean?"

"What do you mean, what do I mean? We were just about to have some fun when I got called in. Then when I got home you were dressed for softball, not the bedroom. You wouldn't let me kiss you. You've hardly said a word. You're so upset you didn't even play along on your show."

"I'm not upset."

"Baloney."

She didn't reply for a moment and then, as she looked at some distant point on the wall she said, "I'm so tired of this."

"Of what?"

"Of you coming home and complaining about your job. And I don't mean just tonight. You knew what you were getting into when you left the newspaper to work in TV."

No, I didn't. But he knew better than to inflame Marti by interrupting.

"But you never stop carping," Marti went on. "You're always griping about TV news being 'news light.' If you don't like it why don't you try to change it?"

"Come on, Marti. We've had this conversation before. It's television. It's not going to change."

Marti faced him. "Then are you?"

Dave flinched and started to answer "no." But then he remembered the conversation with Angela. "What about tonight? I all-but-told Angela I wouldn't call the spokesperson at home or send our reporter to her house. What do you call that? I'm trying to change the way the station does things."

Marti picked up a cushion and slammed it down. "Oh, that's just great. You told your boss you weren't going to do what she told you to." She stood up. "I'm going to bed." Then, turning back to him she said, "to sleep."

"It's only 8 o'clock."

"I don't care." As she walked away Dave heard her say "Good night."

For the next two hours Dave didn't move from his spot, but mindlessly flipped between channels, looking unsuccessfully for a show that interested him. Then he walked to the bedroom door and put his hand on the knob. *Wait. She might be sleeping.* Instead, he turned to the hall closet and pulled out a spare sheet, blanket, and pillow. Taking a whiff, he thought, *these haven't been used for a while.* He took the items to the living room and prepared to spend the night on the couch.

Chapter 4

Saturday morning

The next morning a faint sound from the kitchen woke Dave. Marti was making her morning coffee. The pleasant aroma further roused him and he threw back the blanket and stumbled into the kitchen. Marti was facing away as she sipped her coffee, apparently unaware of his approach. He placed his arms around her waist, expecting her to turn with a sweet smile. But she jumped, sloshing coffee onto the floor.

"Oh, nice going," she snapped. "What do you think you're doing?"

Dave stared at her, then grabbed a few paper towels and started wiping as Marti set her coffee down and left the room.

When he finished he followed her into the bedroom. He knocked on the closed door and called out, "Do you want some breakfast?" No answer.

He shrugged, turned away, and walked to the refrigerator for his orange juice. Later, as he sat in front of the TV eating cereal and watching Saturday morning cartoons, he heard the bedroom door open. He watched as Marti walked to a closet, grabbed a jacket, and pulled it on. "I'm going out," was all she said.

Dave spent the morning by himself, mindlessly flipping between channels. At noon he turned on WERI's news, expecting to catch up on what happened in the Erie area Friday evening or Saturday morning. The station's weekend anchor began the broadcast.

"Good afternoon. I'm Rob Ellis with the latest news. A shocking story from Erie International Airport on this Saturday. A plane made a hard landing at the airport Friday afternoon. WERI has exclusive video of the incident. Our Danielle Patterson is live on scene with the story."

Shocking? What was remotely "shocking" about a plane making a hard landing? Especially since it was more than 20 hours ago?

Dave continued watching as Danielle stood inside the airport at much the same spot Sarah had stood the day before.

"Rob, this is an incredible story. What should have been a routine landing became moments of terror. Watch our exclusive video as this plane comes in." The screen switched to the now-familiar video of the landing. "Despite what you see here," Danielle said in her voiceover, "passengers took the incident in stride."

The same interviews with the Fischer couple as was in Friday's report came on. "Amazingly," Danielle continued, "no one was injured."

"Amazingly?" Dave yelled at the TV. "You're sensationalizing it even more than we did yesterday."

He continued watching the story, noticing that the weekend crew had done exactly what he and Gina had discussed the evening before—used all the same material, but moved the video around and changed the voiceover to make it appear to be new information.

After Danielle finished her on-scene report from the airport the screen switched back to Rob in the studio.

"We will, of course, continue following this story and give you more information as it becomes available."

Continue following? Why? And what "more information?" can there possibly be?

He punched the mute button.

Looking outside reminded him of the upcoming snowstorm. *And besides, what about tomorrow's storm? That's far more important and should have been first in the newscast.* Then Dave reconsidered his words. *Newscast? I mean show, because that story was nothing more than entertainment.*

Turning back to the TV, Dave saw that weekend meteorologist Mike Kowalski was informing viewers about the approaching storm. *Finally.* "We can expect as much as an inch an hour accumulation, starting just after sunrise and continuing to mid-afternoon," Kowalski said.

Now that's news. I wish this storm had hit yesterday so we could have done something besides that stupid airplane story. He mused for a moment. *But would we have?*

In mid-afternoon Dave was still on the couch, mindlessly watching TV, when he heard the outside door open. Marti walked in, muttered a barely audible "hello" and walked into her office, closing the door behind her. Dave considered doing nothing in response, or maybe leaving the house. *No. I'm going to be the better person.* He walked to Marti's office and knocked on her door. "Marti, are you hungry? Can I get you something to eat?"

The response was immediate. A flat "no."

Dave shrugged and returned to his position on the couch, where he remained the rest of the day, except to make his dinner and then to knock on Marti's door again. "I'm going for a walk," he called out. He waited a moment, but heard no response. *No point in asking if she wants to join me.*

Dave slept on the couch again, and when he woke up about 7 he heard the whistling of a strong wind as the snowstorm began.

When Marti got up she continued ignoring Dave, coming out of the bedroom only long enough to pour some Cheerios and milk into a bowl before heading to her office. *I wonder what she's doing in there?*

As was his habit, Dave spent Sunday morning watching the news shows, occasionally getting up to check on the storm's s progress. By 3 o'clock the snow began to taper off, and Dave knew he needed to start shoveling. Normally Marti would cheerfully help, but Dave's only thought was *no sense in even asking today.*

When he finished he came back inside, ate his dinner, watched the evening news and "60 Minutes," and prepared for yet another night on the couch.

There was one part of Dave's normal Sunday routine that he skipped. He couldn't stand the thought of watching another one of WERI's newscasts.

Chapter 5

Monday, 9 a.m.

"Good morning, Lisa," Dave said to his assistant as he tossed his lunch bag on his desk. "Have a good weekend?"

"Great. You?"

"Uummm, okay." He bit his lip and hoped Lisa wouldn't ask for details. He couldn't very well tell her his girlfriend was mad at him all weekend. He changed the topic. "Did you see our stories about the plane?"

"Yep. We played the same crazy video over and over."

He glanced her way. "What do you mean by 'crazy?' The video was wild or we were nuts to keep playing it?"

Lisa laughed. "Both. It's cool video. But the story's done."

Dave nodded. "Yes, I'm glad we're over that and we'll have new stories." He sat down, logged onto his computer, and began his preparation for the morning news meeting, where he would pitch the day's story ideas. "So, besides storm cleanup what's going on today?" he asked Lisa.

"Not too much. There's a news conference this afternoon about the community college proposal. I think we should send someone."

"Agreed."

"And," Lisa continued, "the newspaper published a cute story. A third-grade girl has raised more than $1,000 for the animal shelter where her family adopted a puppy."

"Sweet. That sounds like a possibility. I'll run it by the meeting. Anything else?"

"There was a car crash late Saturday. One person killed. Want to do anything with that?"

Dave thought for a few moments. "I don't know. I read the media release at home yesterday. Saw the victim's name—a guy in his 20s."

His mind flashed back to his days as a newspaper reporter. He would have asked for more details on the victim, what caused the crash, had he been drinking, and many more questions. But he knew his TV station's mindset. A one-car crash wasn't titillating. The dead man wasn't a well-known person. No video existed. "I'll toss it out in the meeting, but we'll probably pass."

At 9:30 Dave walked into the conference room. Angela was already there, along with the usual assortment of reporters, producers, and the web editor. Before Dave sat down or said, "let's get started" Angela spoke. "What are we doing about the airplane landing?"

Dave's head jerked up. "The weekend folks led with it every show, at least the ones I saw."

"I know. But that was the weekend. This is Monday. We have new shows to do. We need to keep on it."

"But there's nothing new."

"That may be, but I still want to keep running it. Look, there's more we can do. We have good video."

Dave ran his hand through his hair. "Whatever you say. We'll make some phone calls." He handed out hard copies of his story ideas. "Here's what else we have."

His colleagues agreed on a reporter for storm cleanup, nodded their agreement on the community college news conference, and "awwwed" over the third-grader.

"Okay," Dave said. "That's three stories. Danielle still needs one. What about the fatal crash?" Angela drummed her fingers on the table. "Do we have any visuals?"

"No."

"Let's skip it then. Danielle's not here until 2 anyway. We'll come up with something."

"All right. We're done then." Dave stood up and headed toward his desk, but heard Angela behind him. "Dave? Step into my office, please." She led the way and motioned him to a chair. "Close the door first."

Dave gulped. He knew what his boss wanted to talk about.

Angela leaned back in her chair and toyed with a pen. "I saw Friday's 11 o'clock newscast. It wasn't any different than 6. You just rearranged the video."

He squirmed. "I know. Remember I told you the airport spokesperson never returned our calls."

"Did you call her at home like I asked you to?"

"No."

"What about sending Sarah and Ben to her house?"

"We didn't do that, either."

"Why not?"

He let out a long sigh. "We talked about this Friday, Angela. I said then that, sure, if we kept bugging her maybe we'd get a comment. But we have a good relationship with her. I didn't want to ruin it by pushing the issue."

Angela didn't reply, but kept her eyes locked on Dave's. He didn't look away, and the stare down continued for several seconds until Angela said, "You should have done what I told you."

Dave did not respond, and his boss frowned. "Do you agree?"

He hated lying, but . . . the word "yes" escaped his lips.

Angela turned to her computer and tapped a few keys. Her printer spit out a piece of paper. "I'm not doing a formal write up." She paused. "This time. But I'll have you sign an acknowledgement about this conversation." She grabbed the paper, glanced over it, and handed it to Dave. It read:

"On Friday, Jan. 19, I asked Dave Wilson to either call the airport spokesperson or send a reporter to her home for comment on a story. He did not do either. We discussed this issue and Dave understands that he should have acted as requested."

Angela handed her pen to Dave. "Sign it, please."

Dave did so and handed the paper back. She signed, opened a desk drawer, and dropped it in. "No one, not even HR, needs to know this conversation occurred, at least for now. But please don't let this happen again."

He crossed his arms. "Okay." Then he hesitated before asking, "Are we done?"

Angela nodded. "You can leave the door open."

Dave swore under his breath as he walked back to his desk. He started to sit, but then slammed a hand down. "I'll be back," he told Lisa.

In the restroom, he kicked a stall door open, sat down, and waited for the tightness in his chest to go away.

◆

Joe Wisinski has been writing and editing more than 25 years. He worked as a newspaper reporter and editor, a radio news announcer, and as the executive producer of a 24-hour TV news station's web site. Wisinski holds a master's degree in mass communications from the University of South Florida and teaches mass media courses as an adjunct professor at the University of Tampa.

 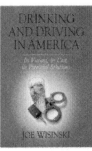  

Buy Joe's books at: https://amzn.to/CL1EMH. Copyright 2021. All rights reserved.

D̲W̲G̲

ELLEN SOLLINGER WALKER

The Before and the After

*B*ackstage always smells the same... Laura thought as she paced back and forth, the floor creaking under her feet...*dust, varnish, sweat, and a little bit of performance anxiety barf.* The red-velvet theater curtains were draped above her head on a thick rusty batten like an elderly woman's housecoat, weighed down, tired, and bitter. In warm cotton gloves, her fingers were what would make or destroy her. For each new concert they faced the *tabula rasa*, a clean slate, and a new chance for triumph or disappointment. Yesterday's performance didn't count, only today's. What was to come was all that mattered.

Her floor-length black dress had been hand sewn by a local dressmaker. She returned several times to be sure the curves and tucks precisely fit. Inside the dress, her heart pumped fast.

But a sharp thread poked her armpit, a thread the seamstress must have forgotten to cut to the quick. It was as annoying as a fly buzzing around her head. *Stop!* she thought. *Think of the music you'll be playing in front of this full house tonight.*

To distract herself, she peered out through a break in the curtain. A row of young children, her piano students in their red-velvet seats, were laughing at something only ten-year-olds would find funny. Andrew, her most gifted student, flipped his seat up and down as he giggled. He was the fidgety one, the "H" in ADHD. But he felt the music intuitively, his scales smooth and shimmering, his arpeggios sparkling, already separating him from the others.

On stage the orchestra concluded a bombastic piece of music with a blast of brass and timpani. About a thousand souls leapt up applauding, whooping, and whistling.

The hall slowly grew quieter, the electricity in the air so palpable Laura could taste metal. *This is it, my Olympic start gate,* she thought. The conductor motioned her onto the stage and followed behind as they entered from the wings.

The 9-foot Steinway, the keyboard giving her a toothy grin, sat on the skirt of the stage in front of the orchestra. She felt the air change from hot to icy cold. Acknowledging the polite clapping, she bowed. What message did the applause send? *We are with you? We love you? We look up to you? We expect perfection? We will be damned disappointed if you mess up?*

She sat down on the piano bench, turning the handle to raise it a millimeter, to draw things out, slow things down. A white handkerchief, like a flag of surrender, wiped the keys. No turning back; no sheet music to lean on.

A cough rang out in the hall, a recognizable hack from her husband Russ, first row balcony; she had forgotten he was there, observing her with his critical eyes.

Laura nodded to the conductor, and the orchestra sounded the first movement exposition, a flip, childish melody in the violins, written by Franz Joseph Haydn in the 1780s. In the *galant* style, the work was composed with a simplicity of melody, harmony, and structure. Laura watched the director's face as he pulled the most out of the string section. Laura placed her sweaty hands on the keyboard, the ivories glistening from the lights above. When she began to play, her fingers slipped around on the keys as if they were made of ice. *At least I'm hitting all the right notes,* she thought.

Into the development section the tension in the music grew, and the principal theme was expanded in alternate and minor keys. More depth here, as if the childish melody of the exposition was suffering some hard knocks. But she held on, riding the scales up and down the keyboard, climbing the trellis of arpeggios, galloping along with a convincing left-hand bass, leaning on the right-hand melody to make it ring pure as a bell.

Then, something was wrong, a mental dissociation. Her hands were moving, her ears hearing the music; but her mind had floated somewhere up into the heavy red curtains. *Concentrate!* she gasped to herself.

But the music went on. The orchestra and Laura arrived at the Recapitulation section as she watched herself play from high above. Her hands still slipped correctly on the keys, her motor memory having solely taken the reins.

On she played, just the movement of her hands, continuing in ontological time. Like a movie that couldn't be rewound, the music happened, fleeting and intangible, here and then gone.

The cadenza was coming, the most difficult part, her playing solo. In the wind up, the orchestra slowed and rested on a chord of suspense and expectancy. The string section lifted their bows to silence. Now, just Laura, alone. She tossed the principal melody around, changing keys, adding octaves, trills, elaborations. Her hands worked like robots, without her control.

But right then, she felt that damn thread poking into her armpit like a taunt. And, *Oh Christ*, it derailed her. At the crucial moment, she missed the goal posts, hit the wall, tripped over the gate, and cascaded down the snowy hill. Her mind returned, and there was nothing to do but fudge it, fake it, trip over the keys, and search for a way out of the maze.

She hit so many wrong notes even the tone-deaf would notice. *My students are laughing at me,* she thought, *and Russ, oh God, how can I go home after this?* Her fingers lost their grip on the keys, she dangled from a cliff, one finger holding on.

Somehow, she arrived at the last, long trill of the cadenza. The orchestra started to play again. They and Laura reached the double bar together, they crossed over the finish line, and found the end.

The music stopped. The hall was quiet. Laura exhaled. Someone coughed. She stood up, wobbling in her pumps. Polite applause began. She shook the conductor's hand without looking at him, then took a required bow towards the audience, the faces a blur of heads. She hurried off the stage, her pumps click-clicking to the wings. No encore bow.

In the faculty lounge, she grabbed her bag with its change of clothes and locked herself in a stall. She ripped her dress off like she was a burn victim. As she tore the dress apart, sometimes she used her teeth, severing the sleeves, rending the zipper from the fabric, snapping threads, tearing away the waist, and splitting the skirt into long strips like black bandages. The black shreds between her teeth were raw meat. She threw all the pieces onto the floor and stared at the pile in disgust, the shreds of black brocade, the fine work of the seamstress, all in a heap of putrid rubbish.

She yanked on her jeans and T-shirt and stormed from the stall, then from the building into the rainy night. She found her car in the employee parking lot, got in, turned the key, and started driving.

Ellen Sollinger Walker is a retired classical pianist and psychologist living in Clearwater, Florida. She is the author of *Just Where They Wanted to Be*, a memoir of her parents' ten-year circumnavigation in their 36-foot sailboat. She also writes short fiction, creative non-fiction, and poetry. She has just finished a novella about unrequited love, *The Hardest Thing to See*. Ms. Walker's short stories have appeared in *The Dillydoun Review Daily*, *Change Seven Literary Magazine*, and *The Pigeon Review Literary and Art Journal*.

Buy Ellen's books on Amazon. Copyright 2021. All rights reserved.

D**W**G

ALEXIS LANGSNER

Gypsy Magic

At my age, which shall remain an enigma, I am still shocked that I am a successful food critic. Nevertheless, and placing aside my website, blog, and a following of 4.5 million on Twitter who love my pointed and precise reviews of famous chefs and all their exotic concoctions, I must confess. When I was a child, I hated food.

It's true, food, when unmarred by human hands, is beautiful. Freshness, color, and proportional presentation can allow the tongue to salivate but my getting-it-down-the-gullet was blocked, unadulteratedly, by a mental sphincter cell that shut down my throat muscles and blocked out the light to any succulent morsel or sweet delectable that had the stamp of "different" on it. In short, the things I ate could be counted on one hand.

Looking back at my childhood, I can say my parents had a lot to do with it. Dad, who was assigned cooking duty in our house, made three recipes: scrambled eggs, a la eggshell bits; lunchbox, white bread sandwiches with palette sticking peanut butter and purple-staining grape jelly; and soggy spaghetti with jarred tomato sauce.

Thank God for Mary Magdalene Olivier. A daughter of Austrian gypsies, she traveled the world sampling traditional and exotic dishes until she settled in a fish shack with her deep-sea diving, fisherman husband. They lived on First Street in Ocean City, Maryland. where my family vacationed every summer, in a bungalow not far from where Mary Magdalene, shall I say, "practiced" her magic.

Mary Magdalene and her husband Ivan, who were both old enough to be my grandparents, called each other the pet names of Mags and Ivy, names they kept to themselves. Her real Austrian name was purported to connect her to some vague branch of Austrian royalty. She allowed all her students, customers, and friends to call her Ma, but reminded all she was not their mother. I was too young at the age of eight to care a hoot about my heritage.

I would never have met Ma at all, except on Saturdays. Dad and I walked our wooden wagon down to the icehouse on the corner of First Street, just passed Ma's place. At the icehouse, big men with dark eyes and blinding, starched-white aprons and smiles that presented still whiter teeth used giant metal clamps to heave about the big blocks of ice. Happy for the 50-cent piece and a returned smile, they slid the blocks over the edge of the warehouse floor and dropped it cold and wet into the pile of newspapers in the bottom of our wagon. Four bits bought ice blocks just large enough to be chipped with a home-sized pick in the kitchen sink. The chips were big enough to hold with both hands as they dripped on your shoes while you sucked on the pointed tip. The rest of them served to keep our bushel of blue crabs and beers cold.

I should note here that steamed crabs were one food group, when combined with homegrown sweet corn and fresh slices of beefsteak tomatoes, that my dad did not have to futz with much to serve. Slathered with Old Bay seasoning, a salt condiment with a kick and flavor to die for, they were pot-steamed live and thrown on newspapers that were masking-taped to the kitchen table. A crab was fully steamed when it turned red and the kitchen smelled like the open sea.

To open a crab all you needed was a small wooden mallet and a small sharp paring knife. It took all afternoon to crack open a bushel, the shells piling up like a miniature hill that was wrapped up in the newspapers after all the crabs were eaten. This ritual was a favorite of our friends, family, and for that matter, the entire state of Maryland.

Opening a crab was where the thrill was. My father salivated over large lumps of white back-fin he thumbed up from the depths of the crab's body as if a treasure found in a sunken ship. His secret finger maneuver was notorious for scooping this delicacy out whole, past the yellow gunk, called mustard, and past the razor-sharp edges of the shell. Voila! This was the prize worth all the other good parts tucked intricately into the crab's body. He'd wave it gently like a trophy-- the crab's back fin far superior to any ice cream cone or lollypop--then sucked on it while telling stories about deep sea fishing with my uncle when his was a boy. Then he'd wash it down with a big gulp of Natty Bo (That's Baltimorean for a National Bohemian beer). I watched his every move and learned to mirror them, step by step. That is how I began my quest for any other food that could live up to back-fin glory.

I began my quest at Ma's. Each time Dad and I walked down the sidewalk to get ice, we passed Ma's brown-shingled, three-story bungalow that crouched over the pavement and was squeezed between the Janey's t-shirt shop and the Barefoot Beachwear Barn.

Before I actually met Ma, I met her rainbow-colored parrot named Squawk. Squawk rarely squawked. However, his huge vocabulary could be heard at the police station three blocks down the street.

"Hey you!" the parrot said, the first time I noticed him. He was sitting on the iron veranda fencing that surrounded Ma's third floor bedroom.

"Hey, look," said Dad. "There's your new third-grade teacher, Mrs. Edwards."

"Where?" I said, my heart pounding suddenly, as if I was late for class. Yet I did not see any grey-haired woman with a cane and a bent back.

"There, perched on the porch above you." Dad pointed up. "Look, she's eyeing you, as if you were a morsel of her lunch."

Lunch, I thought with dread. I was starving. Below, the front door of the bungalow was wide open. The humid summer air about it smelled of garlic, onions, and bacon.

My knees buckled. "Dad, what are we having for lunch?"

"PB and J's, I guess,"

"Not again."

"Come and get it," shrieked the parrot. "Hot pizza pies. Eat at Ma's. Eat, eat, eat your heart out."

From somewhere inside the bungalow, I heard a woman holler, "Shut up, you-mangy-door-stop. You are scaring the customers."

Ma had a yoga and meditation business on her bungalow's first floor. The big store-front window was littered with signs for beginner ballet lessons, yoga classes, and the days she had scheduled to read cards and to tell fortunes.

Her kitchen, which was up the first flight of stairs, took up the whole second floor and looked out over a narrow garden with a moldy-looking green house. A massive tangle of vegetable garden, lay beyond it, as did a small boat dock. The bedrooms on the third floor were loaded with fishing junk and weird paraphernalia which Ma's husband brought back from his sailing ventures to foreign lands.

Outside the third-floor master window (the house was very tall and narrow) was Squawk's domain. She sat like a queen on her throne eyeing the passers-by with shear disdain, primping her rainbow of feathers, clinging to the iron filagree in sunny weather and only conceded to come in when it rained.

As time passed, I grew quite fond of that bird, especially his articulate vocabulary:

Wow.

Spectacular.

Gorgeous.

Come here, cutie.

Kiss me, sweetheart.

Gimme a hug.

Stop it. Don't stop.

Go to Hell.

Bye-Bye.

Dad, though I presumed he disapproved, only smiled and went willingly to the icehouse alone so I could stay at Ma's to observe and listen to Squawk. He preened his feathers, scratched himself with his huge claws, ate big slices of brown apple and stared back at me with one eye.

"Mommy, I just want peanuts and crackers for lunch tomorrow." I announced with batting eyelashes. It became a regular thing for Dad to go to the icehouse and leave me with my well-balanced lunch diet of protein and carbs in front of Ma's. Ma started watching me through the glass showroom window that faced the street.

"Why don't you come in and feed the bird properly," she said. "You are going to spoil her that way."

"Dad says I am not allowed to speak to strangers when I am by myself."

"And how right he is. So why don't we wait until he comes to pick you up and we can ask him if it's okay?"

With permission granted, I stepped across Ma's threshold to find her handing me another brown paper bag, this one with a pretty parrot painted on it.

"The bird food is for Squawk and the chocolate chip cookies are for you."

Ma watched me take a cookie out of the bag.

"What's the matter, Poppit? Never had a chocolate chip cookie before?"

I shook my head.

"It's okay. It won't bite you. Stick your tongue on it. That's what my mother taught me to do, when I first tried any new food."

The taste was butter, melted sugar and something exotic, a flavor from a tropical paradise.

"Squawk adores them, but he's not supposed to eat them. I give him little dog treats instead," said Ma, as she watched me down eight more cookies. "I see you think they are really awful."

"You made these?" I asked. "My mother doesn't buy cookies. If you make them then could you...?"

"Put more chocolate chips in them?" Ma laughed. "Don't fret, Poppit. I will keep an eye out for your dad and we can make some more with more chips. You can take them home for dessert tonight."

~

From then on Ma allowed me to put my tongue on all kinds of new and wonderful foods. She told me stories about their beginnings and about the places from where they had come.

Ma was no ordinary gypsy like the ones on TV who were blonde and wiggled their noses. Ma's hair was coal black and curly as poodles. A big gold loop hung in one earlobe and a safety pin with beads that read "oh please" in the other. Dad loved her layered skirts because she rustled when she walked. He didn't mind she stood taller than him by a full hand's width. When out in the garden she smashed her curls under a straw hat with the words, "OC is for Lovers" on it. She wore lime green high-tops with the toes cut out, she said to let her bunions breathe. When she was teaching ballet and sitting in yoga positions, she wore black tights that betrayed her love of food and men admired. When cooking her spanakopita, and when she washed the dishes, her see-through plastic apron kept water off her clothes.

Dad was always fond of new people and agreed to sit in during her yoga and ballet lessons which he let me take. Ma told him to be as quiet as a mouse and put his ice block in the old tabletop ice box in the back yard. Then Ma taught me the lotus position and other basic ballet positions.

For lunch the first day I was made to walk with her across the beach which was on the other side of the street from her house. We walked along for a long time, for back then the beach was wide and baked by the sun, right up to the jetties where we collected seaweed. This she cooked in her soups on her old blue Aga stove.

It was suggested that I use the tongue dipping method on this soup, which was another food I had never tasted. "This soup has been exposed to one of my cooking spells," she said.

What is a cooking spell like?" I asked.

"Well, I could tell you, but not only is it extremely complicated, it's a secret, meant only for those who eat it with respect and reverence and leave the bowl clean. If you didn't, then I would have to kill you to keep it safe."

She laughed at my shocked stare. Later, she elaborated the spell in great detail, so that no matter what I thought I could remember of it, it would never be something I could cast upon my own cooking years later. While I sipped it and its aroma entered my nose and ultimately my brain, she told me the story of how this soup first came into being.

When she was small, she had a dream. In it she took her little brother on a boat ride atop a choppy sea. The moon was full but the wind grew sudden and tossed storm clouds and their little boat about. This meant that all the makings for dinner got mixed up into one dish and became a hearty fish stew, just like the one I was eating. I was so hungry I skipped the tongue test and went right to slurping up this dark green, slimy strangeness until my belly stuck out. I lay down on her lopsided sofa under Ma's big old patchwork quilt with her English wolfhound, Munch, who snored and nuzzled as I slept, and I dreamed of living on a boat lit by lantern light and a full moon.

~

The Beach was Ma's shopping mall. Shells and sea glass made her wind chimes. Exotic plants infused her enigmatic concoctions. She and Ivan walked, talked and collected while digging their bare feet into the salty shushing waves.

Ivan covered every flat surface of the bungalow with his paintings. The smell of his linseed oil, fresh paint, and Ma's cinnamon spices permeated the cottage air. Little watercolors hung from their doorknobs. Ma's photos of Ivan, holding fish, mending nets and drinking with his buddies littered the fridge. Pictures of her ballet students lined the walls of her studio and parrot pictures blocked the direct sunlight in the bedroom window. Ma snapped one of me standing next to Squawk that dangled like a mobile in the kitchen window. The most stunning of all was Ivan's oil painting of Randy, Munch's father, which hung over the fireplace just across from his busy ink sketch of the sire's puppies wiggling in a basket.

Ma's glassed-in pantry, green house, and little back yard looked out over the small dock where Ivan's small fishing boat bobbed and bumped the dock pole.

"You will find things that make magic in the pantry," said Ma one rainy day. Each side of the room was lined with little drawers. On top of these were glass jars, vases, and blue green bottles, all filled with toadstools, moths, dragon flies, bird feathers, and bones. Others held rings, plastic beads, pebbles, and tiny metal toys. Ivan put some of these in his paintings. Others Ma dried and glued to the walls, like three-D wallpaper. My favorite jar was round-lipped and filled with colorful cat's eye marbles. I could play with these if I ate her radish, carrot, and raisin salad in which she folded her homemade tahini-mayonnaise dressing. I had a dream where I snuck into her house and surreptitiously ate this dressing by the spoonful.

Ma's stories were laden with wisdoms about food.

"Only eat when you are hungry. Pay attention to what you eat: its color, aroma, its shape; its seeds. Never make compost out of food you should have eaten. Just about every fresh food has a shell. Make earrings out of the hard ones."

"No messing around with the ground flaxseed and hemp jars. They are for keeping me regular."

"Regular at doing what?" I asked.

"Oh, all sorts of things."

I took her for her word.

By the end of that summer, I had a pinkish tan, grown an inch, and gained ten pounds. I was proof there was something magic in Ma's cooking.

"I can't help it, Ma, I'm still hungry. I was hoping I could have seconds."

"Oh, well. I guess Squawk will just have to eat your dessert for dinner.

"What? Why? I thought you said everybody has to finish their soup before they get dessert, and I did. How come that means I have to give up my dessert?"

"Everybody ate so much soup already there is not enough left for the parrot"

"What's for dessert?"

"Serial killer cookies."

"What's a serial killer cookie?"

"It's a melted toffee cookie made with Oatmeal cereal.

"Oh," I said, as I weighed and measured the cookie's coconut and toffee gooeyness that smelled divine but were not tongue tested and Ma's soups lasted longer. This was not an easy decision.

"Okay," I said. "How about I save a few sips of my seconds for Squawk and we share my dessert?" I had learned well Ma's skills for negotiation.

"I don't know. Why don't we see what Squawk thinks?"

"Cracker, cracker, cracker," said Squawk. Ma threw him a round white cracker ball that he caught in his beak. The crushed crumbs scattered to the floor as Squawk dove off his perch to gobble them up.

"I guess that settles it then. Seconds and dessert for you, young lady."

I blushed and later offered Squawk a bit of my cookie anyway and then said to Ma, "I was curious about Squawk's cracker crumbs. What sort of cracker was that?"

"Those are Westminster Oyster Crackers. Would you like to try one? Better yet, Poppet. Why don't I make a big batch of homemade Oyster stew, the kind that has my secret magic yogurt and almond cream in it? Ivan calls this ambrosia his favorite. Don't tell Squawk. He adores it, but they are a delicacy he will have to forgo."

"Why?"

"Because he can't eat just one oyster. He will eat them all and then there won't be enough for us. Now, where was I? Oh yes, this stew is called a chowder because it has cream and milk in it."

Uh, oh. Milk was my word for poison. Time tested and unsuccessfully hidden with Ovaltine; it was the toxic antithesis of my favorite candy caramels. That included any food that even smacked of dairy, like yogurt or cream or anything else white and gooey.

"You have to make sure you are really hungry to eat it," said Ma. "We'll let the sun dry out some sea water and use the salt to flavor it. Furthermore, it requires my most potent chant. The tongue test will not work during your participation in this solemn event. This time, you will need to plug in with your nose and your eyes. The best part is you can float little oyster crackers on top of it like little boats. Oh, I can imagine the storms that will toss them on that oyster sea."

Ma's magic was wastepaper compared to my dislike of milk. What was I going to do? I needed to find a way out of this.

I went to Ivan.

"Ivan, what makes you like oyster chowder so much?"

"Did you know the Olympic Gods ate chowder to give them their exceptional strength? The God Poseidon invented it."

"Those gods are fake," I said, but because Ivan said it, I wasn't really sure.

"Ask your father if you can go fishing with us tonight. He can come, too. We'll harvest the oysters and you can see them for yourself. The magic is inside the shells. The story of Poseidon inventing this chowder is one of my favorites to tell. Maybe after lunch tomorrow I can share that story with you. Munch and Squawk love it, too."

"The chowder?"

Ivan threw back his head and laughed out loud. "I meant the story, but they love the chowder too."

I was so excited about going on the trawler I would have eaten shoe leather. I ran home to ask Dad if we could go and he was delighted, too.

Right around my bedtime, when the sun had fully set and a heavy mist had snuck in from the ocean side, we met Ivan and Ma at their backyard pier. The air was thick with wet and a gusty wind had been blowing all day. The lights on the dock swayed to-and-fro.

The boat smelled of gasoline and fish. The floor was slippery. If Dad hadn't been holding me, I would have fallen on the slimy floor. Ivan was wearing a rubber wet suit. Ma was driving the boat. We pulled out onto the water. The boat lifted and dropped. The motor started. Then we were on our way.

Eventually we pulled up a giant net that was dripping with globs of hairy-looking seaweed and swollen with wiggling blue crabs, slithering, silvery fish and lots of crusty-looking oyster shells. Though I was nursing a tight feeling in my tummy, I tried to imagine the magic that lurked within those mysterious bumpy black casings that look more like rocks than food. The mesmerizing lap of the water against the boat held the whisper of dream. Could there be magic inside? Was magic even real? The misty dark and steely boat lights said yes.

When we finally put a foot upon the solid dock, the swaying continued, convincing me further that whatever Ma would make, it had to be imbued with wizardry. But could it make milk taste better?

Then Dad said to Ivan, "I don't know what you are going to put in that soup, but it won't be the magic that makes me like it."

"Oh, I bet you a dollar it will," said Ivan.

Dad jingled the loose change in his pocket and said, "Okay, A silver dollar says I'll be right. I'll try it only because I love my daughter."

The next day, Ma had set the kitchen table with a bouquet of marigolds, coneflowers, and tickseed all stuffed in a tall white pitcher. Places for everybody, including my mother, had been set. Mom said she loved oysters, which was news to me. Dad introduced her to Ivan. Squawk had been brought downstairs as a special treat. Munch sat quietly beside the head of the table. My tummy growled at me about my skipping breakfast.

A briny smell came wafting into the living room from the kitchen. I could hear Ma chanting over the pot. She stepped out for a moment to greet us with her curls punched back by a red bandana and her skirts tangling in the swinging door. "Just a wee bit longer," she said cheerfully. "I'm waiting for the heat to draw out the flavor. Then we can be seated at the table."

It was to say a lot that Dad had even come. Again, he fingered the silver dollar in his pocket, Was it for good luck? He looked relaxed but my tongue was thick and my breath had gotten lost somewhere.

The kitchen door swung open. Ma was carrying a large soup tureen shaped like a fish. She lifted it above her head when Munch placed his nose on her hip. He followed her progress to the table.

The tureen found its place at the table head. Steam escaped. Ivan presented his great-grandfather's ivory soup ladle which his great grand relative had harvested while whaling in Maine. Then Ivan opened the tureen lid and peered inside. He took in a deep breath of the steam and said, "Aahhh." All I could see was the steam, but oh, he was right. It smelled so good.

Then our wide blue bowls were collected and the soup broth was scooped up and allowed to fall gently into each bowl. Carefully and ritually, they were handed back to us by Ivan, one at a time.

My bowl was full of big, soft chunks of potatoes, big blocks of celery, and translucent squares of onion all resting in a creamy yellow bath. The dark grey lumps sat up like ships waiting to dock. Were they the oysters? No one said a word. Then Ma said, "Before you dig in, I am passing the Worcestershire sauce, the sea salt and the crackers, all of which should float on top like little dinghies. And if you look very closely you will see the sparkle of my magic. Can you see it?"

I nodded. I was deathly afraid to break the spell with any more verbal detail.

"Then close your eyes and dip into the sea of the gods."

I couldn't wait. Nothing about this soup tasted like milk. Bacon and melted-butter-toast met my taste buds. Herb-enriched potatoes caressed my tongue. Then something made me think of sitting in little lapping waves sinking my feet in salty sand. It seemed like only seconds had passed when I finished the whole bowl without a drop left. "Where were the oysters?" I asked. "I don't remember eating any of them."

Dad said, "Oh, they were there alright and are now right there in your tummy. At one point, I thought they might come out and tickle you. But they seem really happy down there."

Everybody laughed and Dad gave his silver dollar to Ivan. "This actually should go to Ma, because she was the magician that changed my beliefs about seafood."

So, I found the food that beat Dad's back fin crab meat a lot sooner than I expected. Actually, I have found many foods that meet its equal and go beyond. Yes, there are some things I still will not eat, but most of the time the tongue test suffices in novel circumstances; and yep, I still use the tongue test. Don't tell my competitors. My fans think I have an iron gut. But I tell them what Ma told me: If you can swallow warm milk, you can swallow anything edible.

Alexis Langsner is a graduate of the University of Maryland with a GS degree emphasizing English and writing. She's taken post graduate courses in creative writing at the Anne Arundel County College in Arnold, Maryland. Her short stories have been published in the Amaranth Literary Journal. She is a retired children's librarian and has completed an historical adventure suspense trilogy titled, Men and Angels that follows the life of an Arthurian warrior and his band of men to find the Holy Grail. She recently published an anthology—*The Underlying Thing and Other Stories.*

DWG

NEIL BEDEKER

The Ghost Orchid

Brenda Gonzales had a loving and devoted husband in her Joe. That was until he entered Miami-Dade Central Hospital for a routine hernia operation. A day later he was dead. Whoever said there are no routine operations for senior citizens was proven correct and Brenda Gonzales became very rich. She was already fairly well off from Joe's roofing business. This allowed her to hire a great lawyer, Jack Speers, who got her a 14-million-dollar settlement.

It was early morning and Brenda was in her new greenhouse that she had built on the grounds of her estate last year. It was a major expense but well worth it. For the past few years, she had been kenneling out several hundred of her orchids with a commercial greenhouse. With her own greenhouse, she could personally tend to her orchids. This gave her a purpose in life that she was missing as she approached sixty. She had to have something to do besides tormenting Miguel.

The screen door opened, and she turned towards the handsome young man standing in the entrance.

"I have the Range Rover in the driveway, Mrs. Gonzales," said the grim-faced Miguel as he stood there among her prizes. He was of medium height, but his lanky build made him appear taller. He was very striking with the high cheekbones and the copper- colored complexion of a Native American.

"Yes, Miguel, I trust you had the good sense to fill the tank. The last time you drove me, we had to waste time stopping for gas."

"Yeah, your time is very valuable."

"Are you being impertinent? You know I don't tolerate that."

He immediately regretted he had given Brenda a reason to talk down to him.

"Gassed up and ready to go." He gave her one of those phony forced smiles.

"Come over here," she commanded. "I want you to understand the significance of our mission today."

She walked over to a tree branch that had been pitched vertically towards the ceiling. It was covered with a web of dying roots.

"The orchid looks like a delicate flower, but it is very hardy and adaptive. You can clone it, mutate it, crossbreed it and, of course, create hybrids. There are 60,000 species and at least that many hybrids."

"Very interesting," said Miguel flatly. He hated it when she tried to lecture him.

"Of course, there are always the exceptions," she explained. "That is what we are looking at here. This one was grown from a seed and sold to me. It looked promising at first but now, as you can see, it was a thousand dollars wasted.

Miguel stared a moment at the dying vine. "You paid that for a flower?"

"It's not just any flower. It's a ghost orchid, the rarest and most beautiful."

"Well, this looks like the ghost of the ghost orchid. It's dead."

"I don't need you to tell me the obvious," she said. "The *Polyrrhiza lindenii* is unfortunately one of the species that either lives wild or dies. No grower seems to be able to recreate the environment of the Fakahatchee strand. That is why we must go there today. If your cousin says there is one in bloom, I must have it."

Miguel shook his head. Brenda quoting Latin. If he didn't know his uncle found her dancing in a dive on Ocean Boulevard, he would have sworn she was educated. Hanging around the rich and orchid-obsessed crowd had classed her up some.

"Are you ready to go?" he asked impatiently.

Brenda was dressed in what she was told was appropriate swamp gear. She had a pith helmet with netting she could pull down to protect her from mosquitoes and a long sleeve blouse to protect her arms.

"Did you get the waders?"

"Yes," she replied. "These are really cumbersome. They go all the way up past my waist. Are you sure these are really necessary?"

"I don't know, I haven't been in the Fakahatchee since I was a kid," he said with a shrug.

"My cousin called this morning and reminded me to have you bring them."

"And what about you?" she asked. "Where are your waders?"

"I'm half Seminole. Swamp water won't tan my hide."

"Oh, you're a real tough cookie." She slung the heavy boots over her shoulder and walked towards the door. Brenda paused and looked at Miguel until he took the hint and opened it.

Miguel drove over to I-75 and headed west. The state had placed a sign at the toll plaza officially declaring it "Alligator Alley," a nickname that had a lot of tourist appeal. He set the cruise on 70 and they rode for a while in silence through the endless sea of sawgrass that was the Everglades west of Miami. Except for one gas station halfway across, there were no businesses, no billboards, no signs of contemporary civilization.

"I need you to take me to an orchid show in Miami this weekend," said Brenda, breaking the silence. "If I get a ghost orchid today, I've just got to rub it in."

"Brenda, I'm missing a whole day's work running you around today. I've got six estimates I have to do by this weekend."

Since his uncle Joe had died and Brenda took over the company, she had been making constant demands on his time. Demands that Gonzales Roofing could not afford. Miguel had graduated from high school and taken several business courses at the local junior college. In a company where few spoke English, it was up to him to do the estimates.

After an hour of driving, stands of cypress trees began to appear and the landscape became denser and more wooded. When they entered the Big Cypress Basin, there was a six-foot chain link fence running for miles parallel to the roadway. Miguel noticed the three strands of barbed wire were turned inwards as if to imprison the swamp. The jungle is patient and irrepressible. It was already coming through the fence. Miguel came to Route 29 and swung south on a ribbon of asphalt through the dense undergrowth.

"Where do we meet this cousin of yours?" Brenda finally asked.

"Malito said he would meet us at the tower. That's where the road into the Fakahatchee strand begins."

"Malito," she repeated contemptuously. "I know enough Spanish to know that's not good."

"Oh, he's alright," Miguel assured her. "He got in a little trouble when he was a kid, but my brother Lupe said he's settled down now."

"Well, does this Malito know why it's important for him to be there?"

"Yeah, he's got the picture, no doubt. He's no Boy Scout so you got the right guy to pick a ghost orchid illegally."

"I told you before, Miguel, that the law would do nothing to him if he is a full-blooded Seminole."

"So, you think the authorities will just let him break the law because he is Native American?"

"That's the way the court cases have been going."

"Did you get that from your lawyer, Jack Speers?"

Actually, I got it from my friends in the orchid society, not that it's any of your business."

"Rich folks always seem to know who they can use."

Brenda drew a deep breath of exasperation. "Did you tell him I'm going to give him a hundred dollars? That's got to be a lot of money on the reservation."

"A hundred bucks ain't a lot of money anyplace these days," he replied.

Miguel struggled to keep his mouth shut. *Does she think I don't know how much money she has?* His mind took itself back to the funeral and his uncle's last wishes. Gonzales Roofing employed most of the men of the poor Mexican village of San Teresa where Uncle Joe was born. They came into the country through the Port of Tampa where his older brother Lupe was a big shot in security. The money that they made was sent back to Mexico to support their families. Joe Gonzales had often said that if anything were to happen to him, the company and the responsibility would go to Miguel. He had left a will of sorts. Joe wrote out these wishes on a piece of paper in plain language and signed it. When Miguel presented it at the probate hearing, Brenda's lawyer, Jack Speers, crushed it like a paper cup.

After the hearing, Brenda became a familiar and unwanted face at the office. Before Uncle Joe died, Miguel had never had any dealings with her. He ran the company for his aging uncle and reported only to him. Now, with Brenda in charge, his workload had seemed to double. Brenda was turning him into her personal "gofer", sometimes calling him off the job for ridiculous reasons. Yesterday he had to come in from a job in Homestead, twenty miles away, to get a box off the top shelf of her bedroom closet. That had really made him feel uncomfortable like the guy in that movie "The Graduate."

Any time he refused to come, she would surreptitiously start in with threats to sell the company. If she were really agitated, she would begin talking about having ICE, the immigration people, come in and check out her employees. His older brother Lupe assured him she would not be crazy enough to turn everyone in because it would be the end of the company. He told Miguel she would be shooting herself in the foot. Miguel was quick to point out that Brenda had enough money from the lawsuit, and she didn't need the company. This financial independence made her especially dangerous.

"This is it," Miguel announced as he turned the Range Rover at a sign that said Copeland Baptist Church. Brenda's eyebrows raised as they entered the town of rundown houses and dilapidated trailers. There were no people in sight, just abandoned cars and rusted farm equipment at various stages of corrosion.

"This place looks worse than I remember it," Miguel admitted.

He turned at the street sign for Janes Scenic Drive and proceeded to the entrance to the preserve. An official looking green sign announced they were entering the Fakahatchee strand, but there was no Ranger Station or other sign of life. The only building there had a plaque that said "Fakahatchee Strand Nature Center", but there was a closed sign tacked on the door.

Next to the observation tower there was a rusty eighties' model Ford 150 with both doors open and blasting some funky rap music at about two hundred decibels. There was no occupant.

Miguel and Brenda exited the Range Rover and looked at the truck in bewilderment until they heard a voice calling from the top of the fifty-foot tower.

"Hey, come on up. The view is fine. *Muy fineo.*"

They looked up at the figure dancing to the music on the platform high above them.

"If that is your cousin, tell him to come down here," Brenda said firmly. "I haven't time for nonsense."

Miguel shrugged and complied. "Malito, come down, man. We got to get going."

Malito continued his dancing. Miguel knew it was his way of letting them "cool their heels."

"Malito, come on."

Abruptly Malito turned and came bounding down the stairs three at a time. After turning off the music and slamming the doors of his truck, he gave Miguel some sort of ghetto handshake in greeting and immediately walked to the passenger side of the Land Rover.

"The XR3," he said to Brenda in mock admiration. "Very nice. Does this have the optional high-performance V-8?"

"I have no idea," Brenda said coldly as she stared at Malito without blinking. Miguel winced. The dance for dominance had begun. He knew it was going to be a long day.

"I love the color," Malito said, moving in too close, invading her personal space. "Did you pick it out yourself?"

Yes, I'm quite decisive," she said with a mirthless smile. "I think you will find that out."

"Okay, it's starting to get hot already," interceded Miguel. "We'd better get going."

Malito climbed in the passenger side behind Brenda. *More gamesmanship* thought Miguel. He could talk to her, but she could not see him unless she turned completely around.

Miguel put the Range Rover in gear and proceeded down Jane's Scenic Drive, which quickly became a narrow gravel road. It went fourteen miles into the heart of the Fakahatchee.

So what's with you orchid people?" asked Malito. "It's like you're a bunch of fanatics. Out here chasing around in this God-forsaken swamp for a flower."

"If I have to explain it, you wouldn't understand," she said coldly.

Malito shook his head and continued with his cheerful banter, asking Brenda more questions that bordered on impertinence. She maintained a stony silence.

Malito suddenly stuck his head between the two front captain's seats and took charge.

"Pull off the road to the left up here," he instructed. "From this clearing we can get to the old levee that logging company built. We'll be able to walk on high ground for awhile."

A variety of flying insects greeted them as soon as they stepped out of the Range Rover.

"Welcome to Hell," announced Malito as he made a sweeping gesture towards a stand of dead looking trees. They were drearily draped in Spanish moss and filled with dozens of buzzards. "Those are the gatekeepers."

"So where did you see the ghost orchid?" Brenda asked, uninterested in Malito's theatrics.

"The ghost orchid that I saw in bloom yesterday is about half a mile from here."

"You don't get the hundred until I see it," said Brenda.

"A hundred will get you a look, but I'm not picking that protected bud for that."

"We'll discuss that when I see the quality of the orchid."

"What's ever fair to you, Brenda dear," said Malito putting up his hands in fake surrender.

She had already warned him about calling her "dear". Miguel had not seen his mother's sister's boy in several years. He had not changed. Always trying to control people by unnerving them. Miguel knew that Brenda had danced at some tough joints in Miami before she married his Uncle Joe. He doubted that Malito's macho antics were going to get to her.

She walked ahead forcing Malito to run to take the lead. He sank in up to his knees in the dark water.

"Tannin from the cypress roots turns the water black. You'd better put on your waders. This stuff will rot the legs off a fair skinned lady like you, Brenda."

"If you don't need them, either do I," she declared.

"But I've been here my whole life. I have a good eye for diamondbacks and cottonmouths."

That was the clincher. Brenda stopped to put on the heavy waders. Once she was ready, they forged on knee deep into the swamp. The humidity was already unbearable. The air had the pungent tang of rotting wood intermingled with the sweet smell of a thousand varieties of flowers. Bromeliads like Spanish moss were alive and shimmering in the tangle of trees.

Miguel had not been in the swamp for ten years and had forgotten how alive it was. It was a mass of living organisms battling each other for life. He could not see a square inch where there wasn't a living thing struggling for existence with another living thing. The sound was maddening. The buzz of insects mingled with the chirps of birds causing a constant hum.

Miguel glanced at Brenda to see if she were surrendering to swamp madness. She moved stoically forward with only her darting eyes betraying her uneasiness. The heavy, humid air made it difficult for her to breathe but she trudged forward with determination. He felt a begrudging respect for his seductress, tormentor, dominatrix or whatever Brenda was to him.

"Through here," Malito signaled towards a cypress dome. "The ghost orchid. It's through here."

The dark water was now waist deep and Miguel began to worry about snakes and gators. He had picked up a sturdy branch with a forked end and was using it as a walking stick. It would come in handy if he had to toss a snake out of their path.

"There it is in that tree to the right," said Malito pointing overhead. Brenda moved ahead excitedly and Malito let her take the lead. There was a clearing in the trees and the ghost orchid flew above it like a papery white specter. Its intricate, pouty lips gave it the illusive air of an opera diva.

Each side of the flower tapered into a long, fluttery tail that made it look more of an apparition than real.

It was beautiful and Miguel was struck by God's irony. Why was such a thing of beauty grown only in this dismal swamp where no one could see it? Maybe that was His plan. Only the worthy that had made the journey would be allowed to look upon it. Maybe there was a fairness about it after all.

Brenda plunged forward into the water, her eyes transfixed on the ghost orchid. Suddenly she stopped. She looked perplexed.

"Where is the root system?" she asked suspiciously. "It should be all over the tree."

She had stopped just in time because the next step had no footing. She tried to back up but began sliding into the muck. The water rose from waist high to over the tops of the waders. They began to fill with water and the increased weight was pulling her down.

Malito had begun pulling back from the scene as soon as Brenda entered the water. He had an uncharacteristically tense look on his face. When Miguel looked back at Brenda, he saw her head was barely above the water. Shapes that had appeared to be logs on the edge of the bog began to move towards her. The beautiful flower had been suspended over a gator hole.

"Pull off the straps," Miguel shouted at Brenda. "You have to get out of those waders." He moved quickly towards her and the water was up to his armpits. Miguel held out the branch he had been using as a walking stick.

"Grab hold of this and don't let go!"

Brenda complied as her head began to disappear under water. For a moment all Miguel could see were two desperate arms clutching the branch as she slipped completely under the dark water. He regained some footing and pulled her towards the shallows.

"What are you doing, man?" screamed Malito. "Let her go. You'll ruin it. It's the perfect crime. She'll drown in the swamp. A stupid white woman who had no business coming here."

"You are crazy, Malito," shouted Miguel. "How did you come up with this idea?"

"It was your brother Lupe's idea. He says she has got to go. She can ruin the company. She will get everyone deported."

"Well, nobody told me about this!"

"Your brother said you were weak. You had no cohones. It's time for you to be a man."

"Is drowning a woman what you call being a man, Malito?"

"Let the gators have her," Malito screamed pointing towards the green oval moving in the water.

"It's got to be done now. There's no going back."

Brenda had been in enough tight situations in her life to develop a healthy survival instinct. She somehow managed to remove the shoulder straps and, as Miguel pulled her back, she slipped out of the waders. As she did, the jaws of a twelve-foot gator clenched on the leg of the empty rubber boot.

When Miguel got Brenda to the bank of the alligator pit, she curled up in a fetal position and hugged him. She was shaking and whimpering softly. He had never seen her this vulnerable.

Malito had disappeared. Gone. Vanished. Probably headed back to the reservation where the authorities would have to play a legal "cat and mouse" game to get him. He would have to be apprehended by Seminole Police. Fat chance.

But his brother Lupe. Malito had implicated him. Had Brenda heard? Probably not. She had been fighting for her life. Malito was a fool. Miguel had always felt so. But his brother. He could not let his brother go up for attempted murder. Not just for himself and their family, but for the whole village of San Teresa.

Miguel had simply reacted to the situation in accordance with his upbringing; the system of values that the church and his father and mother had instilled in him. But, as Brenda still trembled in his arms, that hidden part of the brain that shoots out scenarios, right or wrong, let him picture Brenda going under and disappearing. A stupid white woman out in the swamp sucked into a gator hole. Oblivious to everything as she looked skyward chasing a stupid flower. Going under and leaving no heirs. The company would go to his family. Possibly it was the perfect crime.

"Oh, God. Oh, God," whispered Brenda as she pulled away and sat upright on the bank. "That bastard set me up. Your cousin tried to kill me. The ghost orchid was placed there. 'Wear the waders', he said. You might as well have tied weights to my feet and threw me in that pond full of alligators."

"What? I had nothing to do with it. I saved your life."

She looked into his eyes for a long moment, reading him like a poker player.

"You're right," she said resting her hand on Miguel shoulder to steady herself as she got up. "You wouldn't have the nerve to try anything like this."

Miguel stiffened at this comment. For an instant he saw himself grabbing Brenda and throwing her back in the gator hole. His cynical brother Lupe often said that no good deed goes unpunished.

"Let's go," said Brenda tugging on his shirt in the direction of the road. "We have to find a ranger in this hell hole and have them pick up Malito before he disappears into the swamp like the snake that he is."

"He probably already has," concluded Miguel. He walked trance-like holding Brenda around the shoulders. The implications this might have on his family were just hitting him.

"Well, we can get a warrant sworn out for your brother Lupe."

This was the worst case of all the scenarios that were playing out in Miguel's mind. He let go of Brenda and jumped in front of her.

"What? My brother. What's he got to do with this?"

"I'm not deaf. I heard Malito say that this was Lupe's idea."

"That was just Malito talking. I'm sure…"

"I'm sure too," Brenda cut him off. "I'm sure he wants me dead so I don't spoil your little family operation."

Miguel walked in stunned silence the rest of the way to the Range Rover. He got in and it started with no apparent problems. He thought that Malito would try to disable it to buy time. He must have fled in sheer panic.

He found the will to speak his mind as they approached the ranger station.

"Does my brother have to be implicated in this? I mean, he's my brother and besides, it would ruin the business."

"No more supply of illegals smuggled in through Tampa?" she asked sarcastically.

Miguel stopped the Range Rover and looked pleadingly at Brenda.

What do you want from me? I'll do anything but don't turn my brother in."

Brenda looked at him slowly, a coy smile forming on her lips.

"I guess we can start with a more cooperative attitude. I need you to take me shopping tomorrow. We are going to have to buy you the right clothes if you're going to take me to the big orchid show in Miami this weekend."

"But I've got..." Miguel didn't bother to finish the sentence. He slumped forward on the steering wheel and pulled the Range Rover onto Janes Scenic Drive.

Brenda smiled in satisfaction.

Neil Bedeker grew up in the Chicago area and writes historical fiction about Chicago in the 1890s. In his first book, *The Cassidy Posse*, his protagonist, a tough Irish cop named Mike McGhan, travels west to apprehend a fugitive that escaped the Cook County jail. The second book, *Dark Hearts, White City*, is set in 1893 as Chicago hosts the World's Fair. His latest work is *The Outlaw Island,* young adult fare set in post-Civil War Indiana. Neil is a winter resident of Clearwater.

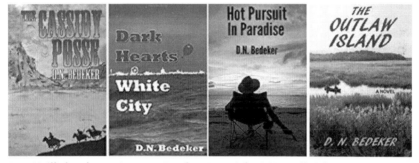

DWG

MARGRIT GOODHAND

Rum and Coca-Cola

Emily keeps wailing while taking turns covering the top of her short brown hair and face with both hands. Her hazel eyes are circled by dark rings and look red from crying. Finally, she says with a frail voice, I really thought he still loves me because he came over about once a week to have sex."

"But the two of you are already divorced?" Anja probes, taking a crunchy off her wrist and tying her blond hair in a ponytail.

"Yes, but I still love him, so I made one last attempt to get him back," she snivels.

"What did you do?" Anja's blue eyes widen while she raises her eyebrows.

"I can't possibly tell you." Emily looks embarrassed.

"Try me, I'm your friend. I'm here for you. You can tell me anything."

"It's awful—I'm so ashamed. Nobody else can ever find out."

"Don't worry. I won't judge you, and I won't tell anyone. I promise."

"Okay, I'll try," Emily takes a deep breath and then starts to talk about the latest personal drama with her ex-husband. "Fred told me that he would probably skip Thanksgiving and sleep the whole day. The other mortician was out sick, and he had to cover for him the nights before and after. Because no one should be alone during that holiday, I had an idea. I stuffed and seasoned the twenty-two-pound turkey I got from work, put it in foil and a pan, took everything to his apartment, and...." Emily's sobbing gets in the way of completing the sentence, and she puts her head down on the dining-room table, grabbing the last bundle of tissues to wipe off her tears.

Anja rises from her chair to get a new box of Kleenex. "You took everything to his apartment, and then what?" she asks.

"I rang the doorbell—I had to ring several times until he finally opened the door, wearing only boxers and a white T-shirt. He just looked at me with these dead eyes and asked, 'What do you want?' I think there was someone in his apartment because I heard a door slam. Anyway, I asked him if I could use his oven to bake the thawed turkey because mine was broken. But he wouldn't let me in. Instead, he called the police who took a report and told me to stay away from him or they would arrest me. One of the officers told him that he could file a restraining order against me—and he did," Emily resumes her wailing.

"That's awful—you know you can always come over to my house if you feel lonely, especially on a holiday. I had a full house, and you know some of the people."

"I know, I know, but it's not the same. I wanted to be with him like the years before."

"Well, I have to go to work now, but you can hang out here until you feel better. Okay?"

"Okay, thank you. I appreciate that."

"Just promise not to contact Fred, or you will go to jail," Anja warns her.

"I won't. Thanks again."

~

Walking through the neighborhood on her way to work at Pizza Italia, Anja passes what a couple of weeks ago had been a fully functioning steel factory. Now it is just a big field with piles of stacked bricks from the torn-down buildings. After she and the other union workers tried to force a pay increase by going on strike, the company just fired everyone no matter how long they, their parents, or grandparents before them had worked there. Then, like pouring salt into an open wound, they hired anyone willing to come back for the demolition.

Anja does not particularly like working under the table at the pizza parlor. But she knows that it is only temporary until she gets a real job that she can put on her resume. Upon hiring, the owner Roberto had warned her to "watch out for anyone snooping around in a suit" and to let them know that she is "just helping as a friend of the family." In the meantime, she figures that what she does is valuable for the economy because of what she recently read. It was "Small business cannot survive in the U.S. without people working under the table."

As she was originally from Sweden, Anja's challenge of mastering vernacular English has increased by working with first-generation Sicilians at Pizza Italia and becoming familiar with some of their daily expressions. Roberto is short and stocky with bushy eyebrows, bronzed skin, small black curls, and symmetrically lined-up white teeth. His wife, Cat, aka Catena, is his first cousin and co-owner of the restaurant.

The same height as, but slimmer than her husband, she shows similarly well-balanced facial features, including an aquiline nose. They look like they could be siblings, except Cat's hair is straight and shoulder-length. Both from Palermo, they are a mesmerizing couple, especially during their loud love quarrels in the kitchen that he usually starts, and she wins. They are at the restaurant seven days a week; however, Cat leaves late afternoons to be home for the kids returning from school, leaving Roberto alone and able to flirt with the waitresses as he pleases.

In the beginning what in retrospect appears funny was embarrassing. Anja remembers her first day at the job when people stood in line at the counter for carryout.

"One-a-slice of cheese," Roberto shouts. Confused as to the meaning, she hesitates until he follows up with two more shouts of "One-a-slice of cheese, one-a-slice of cheese!" Feeling pressured and taking it literally, Anja hands him a slice of mozzarella instead of one slice of pizza with cheese. After that the wailings of "Mama Mia's," rolling of eyes, wringing of hands, and laughter—it was embarrassing. Thank God she is a fast learner, and by now she can not only make pizza from scratch but also prepare all other items from the menu.

Business is slow today. Roberto, while trying to get lewd glimpses of Anja's cleavage beneath the neckline of her red company T-shirt when she bends over, keeps telling her, "Smile, smile, so you get more tips!" Knowing that this will never happen, no matter how much she smiles, because most people in the neighborhood are down and out, she nevertheless answers with a sweet smile, "Yes, boss!"

"I heard Sicily has a sunny climate and beautiful beaches. Why did you leave to come to Pennsylvania?" she asks Roberto while shredding iceberg lettuce, slicing tomatoes, and chopping onions.

"Sicily is very beautiful, but there was no work, no money, no future. Catena had family with connections to the restaurant business in New York. So, we went there first to learn everything about it by working for her uncle, and then we got our own franchise here. One day, we will sell it and retire to where it's warm and where people speak Italian."

"Do you miss Sicily?"

"Yes, especially the climate."

"One day I want to go to a tropical island like Trinidad."

"Why?"

"Because of the beach, turquoise water, palm trees, and calypso." Anja feels uncomfortable telling him more, doubting he would understand or be interested.

Back in Sweden, her now-deceased parents had taught cultural anthropology and ethnomusicology at the University of Uppsala. Both pacifists, they had acquired a vast body of knowledge about the indigenous peoples of the West Indies and Africa. Because their interpretation of that knowledge was a threat to Aryan indoctrination, they had been arrested and forced into Swedish Internment Camps not only for their own protection but also to maintain Sweden's image of neutrality during World War II.

According to her parents, "Calypso is the poor people's underground newspaper with coded messages relating to cruel exploitation and slavery." Today, Anja takes pride in being able to decode music from the Calypso bards such as Lord Invader, Harry Belafonte, Attila the Hun, and Mighty Sparrow. Sometimes she wonders how many people even know about the genocide of ten-million Congolese, and that Mighty Sparrow's "Congo Man" was outlawed in the United States until 1989 because it threatened and mocked colonialism.

Prior to closing, Anja tries to stay away from the kitchen to avoid Roberto, unless there are chores to attend to. Dotti, the other waitress, invites her to take a turn sitting on his lap. "Come on, there is nothing wrong with that. We're just friends here." Anja declines, knowing that it is the right thing to do while feeling like a rabbit stalked by a hungry wolf.

"Come on. You're a boring party pooper," Dotti goads her. "We're just having fun. It doesn't mean a thing. I could sleep next to my man here, and nothing would happen."

"Hey, I am happy to be the party pooper. I let you have all the fun because I like you," Anja responds to diffuse the tension.

Later Roberto sends Dotti home because he does not want to pay wages when there is not enough work for both waitresses. Anja wipes all the tables and counters with extra diligence, hoping he has something else on his mind than talking to her. He has not. As usual when they are alone, Roberto takes the opportunity to vent, and she never knows what might come out of his mouth. While scrubbing the surface griddle of the commercial stove with Ajax, he complains, "I hate having sex with my wife because she keeps her legs closed." He quickly consoles himself with, "There are many other women out there who give me what I like without my even trying." Then he rationalizes, "Sicilian men are machismo. We are supposed to have affairs."

My God—does Cat have any clue what he says about her? she wonders.

"I built a bedroom in the back, and if you are ever too tired to go home or feel lonely, you can stay here—it even has a shower," he boasts while opening the door in the back of the kitchen to proudly show her.

"Thanks, Roberto. It looks nice, but I just live five blocks down the road. I'm too busy to get lonely, and my boyfriend Michael would have a fit," she politely responds instead of telling him what's really on her mind, which would get her fired. And, without having another job lined up, such a response is not a good idea. But, in a sudden flash, she knows how to help Emily to get over Fred.

~

When Anja gets home, Emily is gone. Apparently, she must have felt better. After taking a shower and putting on an oversized T-shirt from Michael, Anja mixes herself a

Trinidad Sour with fresh coconut milk. Then she listens to Lord Invader's "Rum and Coca-Cola" from 1943 performed by The Andrews Sisters in 1945. She puts both hands on her hips and side steps into the Calypso basic with cross step to the tune. The bright voices mock the Creole English. What the island man wrote as testimony had been plagiarized. The demand for alcohol and prostitution are cheerfully endorsed by the sisters. Yet, the song lyrics leave no doubt how exactly the island mothers and daughters provided the supply for the "Yankee dollar."

It's Michael's turn to sleep at the firehouse tonight. She smiles thinking about his dedication. During emergency calls, he will leave her or anyone else on the spot to join his crew. Yet she loves it when he ultimately shows up in need of TLC and is grateful for whatever affection he can get after he's had an especially tough day. They plan to move to Florida in a couple months to continue their education at Florida State University—he for Fire and Emergency Services and she for Psychology. After turning off the light and lying down, Anja's mind drifts to a scene from Emily's last wedding anniversary.

Fred has already moved out. Emily leaves him a message to meet her at the chapel at midnight, the one where they got married. Despite no return call confirming his intent to come, she prepares to meet him wearing a red-feathered black polyester negligee, black-feathered choker, and red stilettos. She waits for an entire hour in the chapel yard, but Fred never shows up. After that she loses it. Back home, she tries to OD on her prescription benzos by swallowing the entire contents of the bottle. Drifting in and out of consciousness while her stomach cramps, she changes her barely functioning mind, calls 911, ends up in the ER, and gets her stomach pumped.

Anja had hoped that perhaps that incident had cured Emily's love addiction. Obviously, it had not, because they had sex again later, which kept her hooked. But now Anja knows what she can do to help her friend; she will introduce her to Roberto, the instrument of her chosen enlightenment, on a Sunday evening when she is off. That encounter will either kill or cure her—Anja hopes for the latter.

The next day she calls Emily, "Hey, just checking on you. How are you today?"

"Better than yesterday at your house. Even though I still miss Fred—or perhaps it's just being married. But I will stay away from him because I don't want to go to jail," she answers and then asks, "How are you?"

"I'm so glad you feel better, and that I won't have to visit you behind bars! I am great—I just got a letter from the Women's Division of the Chamber of Commerce with an invitation to a luncheon where I will be presented with a scholarship check."

"I am so happy for you. Do you ever miss your ex-husband? How long did it take you to get over him?"

"Yeah, I miss him like ball and chain around my legs." Anja laughs, explaining, "It only got easier after I decided that he wasn't worth killing because it would have gotten me a life sentence for pre-meditated murder. I'll never forget accidentally finding under his toolbox a love letter to one of his co-workers. Bonnie Tyler's "Total Eclipse of the Heart" was playing on the radio as I read how he enjoyed their dinner, the wine, the kiss, imagining her in lace, and that she has a nice ass instead of being a pain in the ass. After a week of insanity, all my efforts went into planning an exit strategy with causing the least damage to myself."

"I hope that someday I can be strong like you. I'm not there yet. Will I ever get there?"

"Sure, it just takes time to heal. Hey, do you want to come over on Sunday evening? I'll treat you for pizza where I work."

"Sure, I'd love to. What time?"

"Around seven," Anja knows that business is slow Sunday evenings, and she can easily draw Roberto into a conversation.

~

Anja goes to the restaurant early to have enough time for setting the scene. As anticipated, the place is almost empty. Dotti works alone and tells Anja she can sit wherever she wants. On her way to a back table, Anja peeks into the kitchen. "Hey Roberto, I am waiting for a friend, and I'll treat her for pizza. She is having a hard time getting over her divorce."

"Is she pretty?" Roberto asks in obvious anticipation of a possible new conquest.

"Yes, especially when she wears make-up. I don't know what she'll look like today because she has been crying a lot. Please be nice to her."

"Okay, I will come over to sit with you when she is here."

When Emily arrives, Anja rises to greet her with a hug.

"Hi. I'm so glad you could make it. How are you today?"

"Not too bad. Thanks for getting me out of the house. How are you?"

"I'm so glad you feel better! I'm doing great because of the scholarship I told you about. With that, I will have enough money for a car, so I can get another job."

"That is awesome. You really deserve it," Emily replies, seeming genuinely happy for her.

Angie takes the orders for two Cokes and a large supreme without anchovies. While waiting for the pizza, Roberto joins them at the table, a cup of espresso in his right hand.

"This is my boss, Roberto, the owner of Pizza Italia, and this is my good friend Emily."

"*Femmina bella!* It's nice meeting you," says Roberto, with a big smile revealing his gleaming white canines. Anja hopes that Little Red Riding Hood will learn her lesson today.

"Nice to meet you, too," Emily replies, her hazel eyes lighting up. She clearly enjoys getting attention from a handsome male, instead of chasing after her unavailable ex who keeps dissing her.

Next Roberto flags that he has no intentions to leave his wife, thus ensuring that Emily knows where he stands should she give into an adulterous affair.

"I love my wife, but also love meeting beautiful women like you," he continues. He snaps his right thumb and middle finger while making a kissing sound with puckering lips.

"Thank you for the compliment," Emily answers, her blushing face giving away that she is mesmerized by the Big Bad Wolf, just as Anja planned.

"Women just throw themselves at him," Anja says as she interjects herself between the two. As you can see, he's one-of-a-kind macho man from Sicily."

"From Palermo," Roberto proudly clarifies.

"Right! Hey, how many women have you conquered so far?" Anja baits him with another chunk of meat.

"Too many to count," he wiggles, waving his right hand.

"Just your last two-and-a-half years here in America, a handsome guy like you?" Anja appeals to his ego.

"Many, many." He nods but remains uncommitted to disclose a number.

"Well, thirty, forty, fifty, or more?" She gives him some ridiculous leads.

He bites, "About fifty."

"That's amazing. Hey, do you ever tell your women that you love them?"

"Of course, all the time. Love makes the world go 'round, and I do them a favor by giving them what they want."

"What do they want?" Emily dares to ask, suddenly looking a bit pale.

"Me," he points at his chest and clarifies. "Me, to make them feel better. I know what needs to be done."

"And what is that?" Anja pretends that she does not know.

"I make love to them," he says puffing up his chest.

104

By now Emily's face has turned as white as Florentine lace. She mumbles under her breath, "I don't feel good." Then she gets up and speeds towards the bathroom.

"Thanks for your honesty, Roberto. I think Emily needed to be here today to understand a couple of things," Anja tells him.

"Nessun problema," he replies. "Tell your friend I am here for her if she needs me," he says with a concerned tone and serious face as he gets up and goes into the kitchen.

Emily returns from the bathroom and sits back down, "I don't think I can eat any pizza, I am too nauseous," she says.

"It's okay, you can take it home in a box."

"This guy is a player. He is just looking to get off his rocks," Emily comments.

"Smart girl. Now what does Roberto and your ex have in common?"

"Fred has probably done the same while being with me—Gosh, have I been stupid!"

"Don't judge yourself too harshly for believing someone who has been deceitful. I would suggest though that you stop going to a hardware store to get a loaf of bread."

"What do you mean?" Emily looked puzzled.

"You have to stop confusing love with sex. Love is the bakery and sex the hardware store. During sex, men get something out of their system whereas we women let something in. And if we're not careful, we will walk around with their baggage because sex was all there was."

"Why can't we have both love and sex?" Emily asks in all seriousness.

"We can, but it takes two to get both," Anja responds, just as serious, impressed with her own train of thinking.

"Oh... I think I understand now. For a Swedish girl you are pretty smart."

"Thanks."

~

By now she has a legitimate job as a medical transcriptionist at the local Behavioral Health Center where they provide her with free medical terminology training. The next time Anja goes to Pizza Italia, it is for pick up. Roberto is behind the counter smiling and shouting for everyone to hear, "Anja from Sweden, the best waitress I ever had!"

"Thank you for the compliment, Roberto. Good to see you." She smiles back, knowing he would never say anything like that about anyone who sat on his lap in the kitchen. She adds, "Two slices of supreme, without anchovies, for takeout."

"Stay here to eat. The Coke is on me," he propositions, his smile fading and adding, "I have to talk to you."

"Okay, I guess I do have the time," she replies, wondering at the seriousness of his tone. They sit down in a booth near the window. Dotti is her server. Sipping on his usual cup of espresso, Roberto looks concerned, saying that he has some bad news and wants to ask her an important question.

"Really, what's up?" Anja asks.

"Catena had an affair with Demetri, the Greek Pizzeria owner—my marriage is over," he groans in distress.

"Oh, my Gawd! Did she leave you?"

"No, she is still at the house. She will not move out."

"Don't forget all the affairs you had yourself! Why can't you forgive her?"

"Never. It's different for women. A Sicilian wife can never have an affair, or the marriage is over," he explains, a couple of tears rolling down his cheek. Anja feels almost, but not quite, sorry for him, but for Catena, for sure.

As to the question, Roberto wants to know if she is interested in buying the restaurant at a good price, so he can go into early retirement. She politely declines, stating, "Thanks so much for thinking of me, but Michael and I are leaving Pennsylvania soon. We plan to move to Florida to continue our education there." Roberto looks disappointed.

"Roberto, you are in America now. Things are different here than in Sicily. Try to forgive your wife. Get some counseling. Make some changes," she says, which pretty much ends the conversation because he does not get what he wants.

A couple of weeks later, Anja runs into Catena who tells her that she and Roberto are separated but will not get a divorce "because of the kids." After he had hit her, she hired a lawyer who arranged a meeting with Roberto and the accountant. All agreed that he would move out, and she would run the business. He has relocated to the Dominican Republic and lives in the Italian Colony La Romana.

Margrit Goodhand is a LCSW, author, and sole proprietor of Therapy & Books. She writes fiction and non-fiction. "Rum and Coca-Cola" is her third-year contribution to the yearly **DWG anthologies**. Her first contribution, "Half an Amish Man", was published in 2019. She is the author of *The AOVIA Principle: A Path of Unlimited Potential*, the first chapter of which was published in *The Best of Dunedin Writers Group 2020: An Anthology.*

Buy Margrit's book at **www.therapynbooks.com** or **Amazon.com**.

DWG

HELEN DIBBLE GOCHIS

Eleven Moons

The Bridge of Dreams and The Bridge to Ul Tyma

In January 2020, no one on Earth was prepared for how the Covid-19 pandemic would relate to decisions of the past, cast light on the social problems of the present, or create consequences in the future that are described in Eleven Moons-The Bridge of Dreams. New York City reporter Maya Stone trusts fate when, as a single woman, she opts to use an unorthodox method to have a child. Her dreams during her pregnancy are filled with visions giving her insight into her ancestry and questioning her choice of core values.

The dreams bring clarification to historical events—some leading to harsh realities facing the world during the opening year of the coronavirus. The second book in the trilogy, Eleven Moons-The Bridge to Ul Tyma, begins in August 2020 with the introduction of the planet Ul Tyma and Maya's unique child, Luna. The following are excerpts from the beginning and the last chapter. Look for Eleven Moons-The Bridge to Life in the next Dunedin Writers Group Anthology.

PRELUDE

The planet Ul Tyma emerged from the debris of the Big Blast four billion years ago. It is located far beyond Earth's outer solar system, well past Ceres and the asteroid belt, and separated from Earth's galaxy by a space only penetrated by the rays of the powerful sun. Ul Tyma is a celestial body in orbit at a distance not yet discovered by the mechanical eyes of the astronomers of Earth.

Maintaining the balance of the Universe is of paramount interest to the wellbeing of Earth and Ul Tyma. It has become clear that problems on Earth are threatening to shatter the fragile equilibrium. The actions of the people are intricately tied to the symmetrical balance of the scale and the swerve of the needle has been keeping that tenuous balance in check. The coronavirus pandemic has now brought deeper swings and more fearful emotions to the thoughts of the people of Earth. It is the duty of the Elders of both planets to receive the thoughts with the internal feelings and intentions of the people of Earth and to filter back those thoughts of good conscience, while not interfering with the free will of the people.

Elder One of the planet Ul Tyma has called for a meeting of the members of his Council regarding the consequences of the escalating negative thoughts of the people of Earth and the implications for their own planet.

The four Council members have prepared to receive the mental communication from their leader by clearing all other thoughts. No one is sitting around a board room table chatting while waiting to be called to order, no one is late for the meeting, no pads or pens for writing notes, no coffee in polystyrene cups.

Elder One of Ul Tyma begins:

"It has been more than seven Earth moons since it was determined that the coronavirus pandemic was to have a threatening capacity for widespread global infection. My counterpart, Elder One of Earth, is concerned that their scientists have yet to find a medication to affect a cure, or develop a vaccine with any assurance of its efficacy to stop the spread now and prevent a recurrence of the virus. The question for us is to determine how the planet Earth's problems today might have an effect on our planet in the future and what we must do to protect Ul Tyma."

The Elder of the South, always optimistically encouraging hope and new beginnings, gave his view of the situation.

"We must not consider Earth's problems our own. This pandemic will pass as all the others have. It may mean that changes have already occurred that will accelerate the demise of this particular Earth civilization, but the alterations will be gradual and as at many times in the past, it will be buried in history and memory as a new civilization rises."

The Elder of the East is interested in any movement on Earth that would have a consequence on Ul Tyma and is always making an effort to enlighten the Council. Usually expounding on obscure historical events and embellishing them with minute details, he often went on longer than the other Elders were comfortable with.

"We Elders of Ul Tyma are well aware of the people of Earth's curiosity about the outer space surrounding their planet. We know about the legends of thousands of years ago that told stories of winged chariots and magic carpets and the flying machine drawings of Leonardo De Vinci. The most repeated legend was first described in 43 BC by the Roman poet Ovid, when Daedalus and his son Icarus set out with wings of feathers held in place with wax and the boy flew too close to the Sun. The heat melted the wax and the feathers loosened, sending him to Earth."

Expecting encouragement for his knowledge and sensing instead sighs of impatience, the Elder of the East continued his thought with a bit of sarcasm.

"Perhaps, while enjoying the initial success of his flight, Icarus forgot the warnings of his father and ignored his words of caution—mythology often has aspects of the reality of present times."

The Elders had long ago assured themselves that although interesting, Earth's problems and experiments going into space hardly concerned them and Elder of the East's comments did not disrupt their calm demeanor.

The wise Elder of the North summed up their thoughts.

"We were well aware twenty Earth years ago when an international effort launched astronauts to a modular space station in low orbit around their planet. They were of interest for their courage, and we had taken due note of Earth's scientific advancement. We were also aware that footsteps of Earth people have been recorded on the moon, but the prideful competition between countries on Earth has ended with failed missions and financial exhaustion."

The signs of impatience became sighs of relief. Frustrated but determined to educate the elders and stir their interest in his fears, the Elder of the East went on to elaborate on Earth's present obsession with space exploration.

"In the sixth month of this year on Earth, NASA, the discarded National Aeronautics and Space Administration, was revived by a private venture called SpaceX that launched two astronauts into orbit headed to the space station. There are plans for expanding and lucrative funding is available.

"There are four Rover expeditions in space now manned by artificial intelligence looking for signs of life on the moon and on Mars. Pluto, which is near the asteroid belt that our scientists consider in proximity to our planet, has been closely observed.

"Using artificial intelligence and machinery Earth has perfected, there have been targeted deadly attacks on conceived enemies at huge distances with incalculable scale and speed."

The usually reticent Elder of the West interrupted to express his dark thoughts.

"In light of the information presented, there should be concern among us regarding the possibility of a more potent viral recurrence on an even larger scale being inevitable in Earth's future. It seems clear that Elder One of Earth and our own Elder of the East are warning us of the danger that the next virus with the capacity to do even more damage would bring the leaders of Earth to seek out a habitable planet to take over."

The Elder of the West continued expressing dark thoughts that seeped into the minds of all the Elders.

"Relevant to the present pandemic crisis and imbalance of the ruling forces on Earth we must conclude that with their massive weapons and aggressive attitude coupled with more advanced space exploration, Earth would present a real danger to Ul Tyma."

The effect of Elder of the West's thoughts on the probability of Earth reaching their planet aroused the fears of each Elder. In an instant all of them expressed anxious thoughts wanting assurance of Ul Tyma's military capability to thwart the imminent danger.

To Elder One it was not unlike a Zoom meeting in the sky—one without pictures but with words flowing like electricity in a lightning storm. The thought of buzzing bees flashed through his mind. Attempting to still the tempo of the conversation, he reminded them that the role of all Elders was to be aware of the thoughts of the people and to reflect positive thoughts in all negative situations in an attempt to maintain the balance of the Universe.

As calm ensued, Elder One of Ul Tyma informed them that his counterpart, Elder One of Earth, was working on a plan to forego any danger to Ul Tyma while continuing in the primary mission of all Elders.

"We have set a lapse of time until the last full moon of this Earth year 2020 to reassess the danger to our planet from Earth. Any plan will require contemplation and must be agreed to by all before action would be taken to go forward."

DECEMBER 2020

The Elders of Ul Tyma have been waiting to receive the plan intended to still their fears of Earth violating their space. Their thoughts range widely as they share them and take note that the Earth moon of December is about to rise indicating the end of the waiting period.

Earth's action regarding the coronavirus has been confusing. The global pandemic is being treated as though it is a phenomenon to be dealt with by each nation often choosing to ignore the rules of isolation with lines being drawn flaunting cooperation and the good of the whole.

The leading country of Earth is embroiled in a war within its borders. They maintain that this is simply politics, but the arms carried everywhere, and the threats of violence prove otherwise.

There are basic differences that have been festering for generations and are coming to light. These differences are rising to the surface and receive much attention for short periods of time but arc not being addressed.

As for our anxiety that they might discover our planet and change our way of life, there is little chance of that. They do not wish to escape their problems as we suspected. Their interests in space are tied up in paper money. Wealthy people have given millions of dollars as a deposit for a future trip in space around the moon. Advertisements for a ten-day vacation on the moon with an average cost between fifty-five and eighty million dollars are appealing to billionaires who hope to live long enough to achieve being among the "first."

Their sights are not set beyond the Moon and Mars. Our species has evolved by seeking new pathways to create optimum balance. Shared intelligence can alter thoughts unless the information sent by outside forces is controlled by fundamental morals.

The morals of the innocent, evident at the birth of man and nurtured by connection to the Earth and dependency on the group, must be retained. Human development was guided by adapting to constant change and maturing without losing that genetically inherited innocence. Essential elements for balance are not presently evident on Earth.

The continued regeneration of the Universe requires man to continue to protect its very existence to maintain the required balance. The forces of nature can be both a generous guide and a formidable foe, but nature and man both ride the scales and balance can only be achieved by their actions in unison.

"Am I to conclude then that we are agreed that we must continue to assist the Elders of Earth until the time in the future when the people of Earth have achieved the balance required?"

"Agreed."

"We will ask the people of Ul Tyma to send thoughts of love and good will through the universe to the people of Earth in a continuous stream of the beauty of nature, the richness of life—a bright light to pierce the darkness."

The serious consequences of the pandemic have alerted the world. It is in the power of the people of Earth to contain its further spread.

"Is it agreed also that we will continue to learn from Earth that the balance can easily sway so gently that no notice is taken for generations until man stands at the precipice and does not comprehend the consequences?"

"Agreed".

"We shall not require any shield or defensive weapons against Earth at this time?"

"Agreed."

Luna is distraught. She has been lonely in her thoughts for days shutting herself off to both Elders since losing the ability of mind-to-mind communication with her mother. It was for such a short period of time while Maya was unconscious.

"I have no wish to see anyone, but as an infant my parents control my every movement. Chelly will understand my disappointment—she shared many moments with mother and the Elders. This is a celebration of her birthday and I must congratulate her.

"Friends and family have gathered at Grandfather Shaman's cabin to honor Chelly's third birthday and to welcome and celebrate Maya who had recovered so well from her coma. Prayers of gratitude filled the room with blessings for both Maya and Chelly. There were several presents that Chelly joyfully unwrapped, and she graciously thanked everyone. Smiling, she bent over Luna's carrier and Luna responded with her thoughts and waited for Chelly's usual mental response.

"I guess birthday wishes are in order. Sorry that I have been distant, but I am sad that we both lost the path to my mother's thoughts. At least we still have each other."

Luna looked into Chelly's bright and shining eyes, but her mind received no message of recognition, only a smile and a kiss on the cheek. Her disappointment was great. Suddenly she was isolated and felt a loneliness she had not known before. Bewildered, she watched the moving lips, heard the sounds all around the room and realized no thoughts were directed at her. She reached out to the minds of the Elders—now her only means of communication.

Elder One of Earth begins sending thoughts of soft music and remains quiet as Luna unburdens herself.

"My destiny as a harbinger of better times is a twist of fate that has proven to be my worst dream of all, a nightmare.

"My mind has been filled in preparation for a part in a drama that my youthful body is unable to play. Children have no voice that is loud enough to be heard over the din of the world's problems and the minds of adults that are not open to negotiation.

"I stumble to keep my own balance and have barely learned to manipulate the fingers on my left hand and my right to cooperate with each other. The people of Earth are already proving my task impossible.

"Insults, curses, threats and bombs have infected the fingers at the ends of the arms of the world. One arm rich one poor, one right one wrong, one black one white, one starving one gluttonous, one red one blue, one too far to the left the other too far to the right—limbs so far apart they will never reach each other.

"The bubbles of man's greed, like those in boiling water, rise and then burst, leaving only the desire for more intact.

"The word *civil* defies its synonyms of *chivalrous, courteous* and *polite* and gives no clarity to *relationships between citizens*. When *civilizing* Native Americans, it meant *bringing out of a savage state*; Roman soldiers and chivalrous knights *civilized* the barbaric societies that worshipped a different god; during the American Civil War slaves were either property to be defended or humans to be made free. Revolutions leave blood in the streets that can never be cleaned. Civil liberty can mean the right to be armed, freedom of speech, or have no meaning at all to many people.

"Where is the change I was to bring about? When am I to be this harbinger? I am in the youth of my life on Earth and each day flies away."

~

Exhausted after transmitting her thoughts, Luna cries loudly. Everyone assumes the cries are pangs of hunger but

Elder One of Earth knows her very real pain and sends this message to comfort her.

"The thought that time marches on is inaccurate. Time and change creep at a pace that man can only see when looking at what has already passed.

"Those are the lessons of history—but Earth is now at the point where change is in the hands of man and their minds have moved from the simplicity of life and nature to a more complex movement which has upset the tenuous balance of the Universe. You do not yet understand the importance of your life and why you were chosen.

"Challenging change and the balance of the Earth is too great a burden for a mere child to bear. Any hope of balancing the nature of Earth is gone."

Elder One of Ul Tyma has also been receiving Luna's thoughts and sends a message of hope.

"The Long Nights Moon of December 2020 is in full brightness and the Elders of Ul Tyma wish to thank you and to relate to you the considered thoughts of our Council after much deliberation.

"We have concluded that there is no imminent threat to Ul Tyma that would bring any necessity to defend or arm on our part.

"As you point out, Luna, Earth's problems may not be surmountable for many more generations and harmony and balance may never be achieved. We understand your frustration and acknowledge the veracity of your dark thoughts.

"We have examined carefully the present and the past and do offer hope. Going back more than three thousand years before the present calendar when the years were encrypted in stone, the predictions were clear.

"The Spirit of the Jaguar prevailed for thirteen centuries before there was darkness. The energy of the Wind gave rebirth, and the next era of the Sun lasted another seven centuries before the Winds became hurricanes and there was a fourth Sun, the one of Fire. The Fifth Sun has now lasted for thirteen centuries and it has been predicted that it will fall, and a new Sun will rise, the earth will survive, and the new Sun will warm it as always.

"Perhaps now the end will come with lava exploding from the center of the Earth as predicted. My life on Earth looms before me as a difficult one. I don't want this blessing of sensing thoughts.

"Ul Tyma seems a paradise and I know that I can ride the stars. Let me follow my ancestors. Please guide me through the dark sky so that I might reach Ul Tyma safely before the bridge is gone."

EPILOGUE

"You let your affection for the child keep you from telling her details of the final prediction.

"You know well it was predicted that the fifth Sun would be destroyed when the solar system would align with the black hole at the center of the galaxy. The magnetic poles would sweep and switch and falter leaving the atmosphere to be stripped away by a devastating solar wind. The planet Nibiru would collide with Earth and turn solid ground into a spray of magna drifting through space.

"Our special child, like Chelly, may reach the age of three and enjoy her life without the memories of failure. However, her work on Earth may not be done. We shall see if Luna truly is a gift from the gods while keeping in mind that they are both quite unpredictable."

A member of the group for the past six years, Helen published her first novel, "Animec," at the age of 83. She followed shortly with "Katerina," a nod to her parents' native Greece, and then wrote "Quincy Finds the Library" to help third grade readers. In "God Meets Zeus," she questions myths and truths as she follows twelve modern day youth in making life's decisions. Her latest "Eleven Moons" series highlights the moral state of the world during the coronavirus epidemic. www.helendibble-gochis.com.

Buy Helen's books on Amazon Books. Copyright 2021. All rights reserved.

DWG

SUSAN ADGER

Saying Goodbye

Wisps of grey smoke drifted skyward while the burning book crackled in the heat as it was slowly transformed into ashes. I sat beside it in the grassy yard, watching, feeling the permanence of the loss, regretting things I had not said or done and lamenting others I had. A book, *Stranger Beside Me*, the story of a serial killer, was typical of Donovan's choice of violent, rage-filled reading material. It was a purchase I hadn't wanted to make, but he was my son's best friend and I'd taken him to the bookstore and promised to buy whatever he chose. That's what he wanted for Christmas.

A few months later, in Fairbanks, Alaska, at 4:00 on a frigid gray Sunday afternoon, alone in the cellar of a friend's home, he put the barrel of a gun in his mouth and pulled the trigger. He was twenty years old. It was the first day of spring.

My eighteen-year-old son, Timothy, called me from Anchorage at five the next morning, sobbing, and told me he'd just heard what Donovan had done. I was stunned. I couldn't believe it. I didn't want to believe it. I asked Tim if he was all right. He said no. Then I asked if he'd talked to

Debby, Donovan's mother. He said the police were going to notify her. I'd met Debby only a few times but knew her life hadn't been easy. Donovan had told us she'd been diagnosed with mania and had been on strong medication for decades. He'd never met his father.

About ten that morning, although I dreaded doing it, I called Debby from work. "Hello, Debby, it's Susan Adger."

"Hi there, Susan." She sounded totally calm.

"How are you?" I asked.

"I'm fine. How are you?"

I didn't know what to say. Did she not know about Donovan? I was stunned into silence.

Finally, she said, "I'm glad to hear from you, but why are you calling?"

I could hardly speak. "Oh, um... Timothy called early this morning," I said, panicking. Then, after a pause, "There's been an accident."

"Oh no," she said, instantly terrified. "Is Donovan okay? Did he get hurt?"

"Well, yes. He did get hurt, but..."

"What happened? Was there a wreck? Will he be all right?"

She was supposed to know! The police should have told her! I couldn't think of what to say. Another long pause. "Is anyone there with you?"

"No," she said. "What happened, Susan? You're scaring me. Is he alive? Is he all right?"

I knew you should never give anyone news like this when they're alone. I took a deep breath, my brain went blank, then I heard myself say, "Well, no, Debby, he's not."

"*What do you mean? WHAT DO YOU MEAN?*" she screamed. "He's not alive? Is he dead? What happened? Was he in a wreck?"

I broke out in a cold sweat. My stomach knotted. I wanted to throw the phone down and run away. But what came out was, "No, he wasn't in a wreck."

"What then? *TELL ME! WHAT?*"

I couldn't tell her. I just couldn't. But I had to. If only I'd known the police hadn't notified her. If only… "Well… well… he committed suicide."

Howls of pain erupted through the phone.

"Debby… Debby, listen to me. Please, Debby."

Through her sobs she said, "I'm gonna call Pete. He's at work. He'll come over."

"Yes, yes," I said. "Call him right now. And call me right back and let me know he's coming." I hung up the phone, horrified at what I'd done. You never give somebody news like that when they're alone. Especially over the phone. NEVER. I knew that. I should have put her off, lied or something until someone else was with her. I'd have left work and gone to her, but it would have taken me forty-five minutes to get there and Pete would be there long before then.

She called back a few minutes later and said he was on his way.

~

Damn it, Donovan! You asshole. How could you have done that?

No, he wasn't an asshole. He was an innocent, abused child, a lost soul. And he'd done his best.

Over the following months my grief seemed to dissipate for periods of time, then suddenly leap up out of nowhere and slap me in the face. When I saw a red Land Rover driving toward me on the street. Or when I glimpsed a dark, handsome young man, with wavy black hair and wire-rimmed glasses, a five o'clock shadow and a particular tilt to his head, sitting in a restaurant booth. Or I ran into a photo of him, playing a guitar while Tim played the drums, which they did for hours on end at every opportunity.

I don't know how a mother ever survives this. Debby's pain could not be less than his.

~

When Donovan was sixteen, he'd lived with me and my three kids for about nine months and had been in and out of our lives ever since. His boundless nervous energy often caused him to pace the floor as he carried on a conversation; even when he sat, he was in constant motion. His quick mind and drive to succeed led him to think too hard and plan too much. His resiliency was remarkable; sometimes he seemed to bounce back from problems that would have defeated others. What little sleep he got was punctuated by nightmares and his ever-ready temper got him fired from many jobs. He was outspoken in stating his belief that all human beings are untrustworthy. Once when I happened upon him sleeping on the sofa, he was curled in a fetal position, his thumb in his mouth.

He'd moved back in with me again before he'd left to join Tim in Alaska. During that time, I did my best to get him to go to counseling, but, of course, he wouldn't. This time, I had taken him in somewhat reluctantly because my own children had left home, and to my surprise I was enjoying my empty nest. The two weeks he planned to stay stretched to three months. I was pleased when he started preparing to go on with his move.

He seemed to feel really good about getting off to a new start and said he'd even made peace with at least some of his enemies, unusual for him. He sold most of his belongings including a bag of his clothes and instructed me to give the rest to the Salvation Army. Since he was taking the bus to Alaska and didn't want to have much cash on him, he left $500 with me to send when he needed it.

That money later helped pay for his memorial service.

After his death, I thought of him constantly. I cried too many tears and regretted too many things for too long and it wasn't getting better. Why hadn't I seen how desperate he must have been? And the thing about making peace with his old enemies… it was such a red flag. Getting rid of most of his clothes. I should have seen it.

I wished I hadn't complained so much when he fell asleep on the sofa, leaving the lights and the TV on all night; or when he cooked more food than we could eat so that most of it grew moldy in the fridge. If only I hadn't resented his intrusion.

I decided to take something he'd left behind and completely, absolutely erase it from existence, perhaps symbolically easing my oppressive feelings of guilt and loss. I chose fire, the ultimate purifier, because it destroys all that lies in its wake and lays the foundation for new growth.

I dug through a box of Donovan's things - many overdue books from the library- as well as books and audiotapes he'd bought on philosophy, true crime, and get rich quick schemes.

And there was that damn book I'd given him for Christmas.

I took that gruesome book, a hammer and some matches, and went to my backyard. I sat cross-legged under the blooming Jacaranda tree, surrounded by fallen purple petals; tears came to my eyes and rage rose in my heart. Goddamn him, that fucking asshole. How could he have done this? Clenching the hammer with both hands, I raised it high over my head and slammed it down on the book. It bounced back at me. Why did he? I hit it again. How could he? And hit it again. Why hadn't I… The book flipped open. I hated him. I continued beating it, turning the hammer claw-side down, lacerating the book with every swing. The binding split apart. One section and then another ripped loose and fell to the side. I hit and cried and hit and cried and hated him and loved him.

When I could hardly lift my arms and the tears were cried away, I stopped. I felt calm and unclouded. For a quiet moment I sat, wondering how he felt at the end. Angry? Afraid? Peaceful?

Slowly I took a wooden match from its box, lit it, and cupping my hands, placed the flame under one of the tattered sections of the book. At first it burned slowly, curling the edges of the pages in a graceful orange glow. Gradually it began to crackle, and pale-yellow flames began releasing its earthbound energy to the clear blue sky above. I sat there with it. When the fire began to ebb, I poked at the remaining pages with a stick, igniting the unburned portions.

Then I leaned back, my arms around my knees, and watched the smoke dance on an agitated breeze. A little boy walking on a nearby trail with his father said, "Daddy, I smell a campfire," and I smiled.

As I watched the pages disappear, I could feel Donovan beside me, in jeans, shirtless and barefoot. He was sitting in the same position as I, his dark hair curling around his handsome face, watching the fire. He was still for once, and seemed peaceful. As the book burned, morphing into vapor and ashes, it came to me that Donovan, too, was transformed from a tormented existence, hopefully, to freedom. I was clearly aware of the innocent child he had once been and perhaps was now again.

When the pages were gone and the last whiff of smoke had struggled skyward, in some way I understood that when matter ceases to exist in one form it is manifested in another. Life and death are but the ultimate symbols for holding on and letting go.

I accepted Donovan's choice and promised myself I'd stay in touch with Debby for a while. And, at least for the moment, I forgave myself for not being able to save him.

The following week I took Debby out to eat on my lunch hour, and we continued to meet every few weeks.

Three Years Later

As Debby opened her front door that cool January day, a light breeze blew her sparse, blonde, frizzy hair into a halo, making her look as if she was being electrocuted. She grinned, bright red lips framing the false teeth she'd recently obtained from the county's dental clinic. She leaned forward and said, "Come in, Susan. You look nice."

I hugged her and entered, passing the new iguana in his aquarium next to a three-foot stack of unwrapped newspapers. An aluminum folding chair faced the window. Beside it, on an orange crate, sat a heavy round green ashtray with at least two dozen cigarette butts placed meticulously around its perimeter. Pachelbel's *Cannon in D* blared from the boom box beside the chair, replacing the Metallica she'd seemed to play constantly until the last couple of months. I used to worry about the noise the old iguana, Doc, had to contend with. It would have driven me crazy. I wondered if the new iguana, Stimpy, liked Pachelbel any better.

"Hey, Susan, I like your vest." She leaned forward and touched the hem of my latest purchase. "Come on in, I'll get the drinks." I followed her through the orderly living room, decorated with six or seven plaster casts of human skulls in various sizes, some wearing straw hats or baseball caps, others were bare. Posters of Metallica and Alice in Chains graced three of the walls. The fourth wall was completely covered with a huge TV screen and the latest in stereo equipment, but those belonged to Pete, and she was not allowed to touch them. Eight years before, when they were still lovers, he'd been appointed her legal guardian because she kept spending her entire disability check the first week she got it. That relationship had since deteriorated into a strained friendship. Now he was legally married to a woman who lived an hour away, whom he visited on weekends. The rest of the time he lived with Debby.

In the dining room I placed two Styrofoam containers of food on the table.

"I'd have poured your juice and put it in the freezer if you'd phoned before you came over," she called to me from the kitchen. "That way, it would have formed ice crystals while you ate. Do you like cherry? I added some cherry juice to the apple. Makes a nice color."

"That sounds good," I called back. Atop the small dining table was a wooden stand in the shape of a bare tree on which was perched a stuffed mongoose wearing sunglasses. I moved it to the floor, then pushed the Styrofoam container with her chicken sandwich to one side and my Greek salad to the other. She placed two frosted mugs of juice on the table, then, thankfully, went to the porch and turned down the music.

When she returned, she stopped at the bookcase that held all she had left of her son and said, "Look what I did. New frame." She held up a picture of Donovan, a copy of one I'd had enlarged for her, and my heart clenched as it always did when I saw that photo. He was wearing a blue denim shirt and baseball cap and he needed a shave as was the style in the early '90s. His darkly handsome nineteen-year-old face was arched back slightly from the camera, and he was peering down through wire rimmed glasses, giving us that familiar, engaging smile. Those glasses were now kept on the second shelf of the bookcase, tape from an old band aid still on the nosepiece.

"Nice frame," I answered. "What kind of wood is it?"

"I don't know. It's dark. Walnut?" She rubbed her fingers lightly along the edge and returned it to the bookcase.

"By the way," I say, "Remember when you gave me some of Donovan's ashes?"

"Yeah."

"Well, when Tim was home for Christmas, he took them back up to Alaska with him. He and some of Donovan's other friends took them up on a mountain where Donovan liked to go and scattered them up there. He said they had a little ceremony, played guitars and sang some of the songs that Donovan liked. After talking about him for a while they scattered his ashes up there. He thought Donovan would have liked that."

Sometimes I asked myself why I still visited this woman with whom I had nothing in common but her awful tragedy. Her phone conversations were long and tedious. Sometimes I didn't answer her calls. Sometimes I didn't call her back. Maybe I kept in touch because it reminded me how grateful I was that the most terrible thing that can ever befall a human being had not happened to me. Or maybe it was the times Debby's hard-earned wisdom shone through her mental illness and surprised me.

"Come on," I said. "Let's eat."

She sat down and opened her Styrofoam container. "Yum, chicken breast sandwich. Hey, look. What's all this?" She lifted the edge of the bun.

"What?"

"It's got lots of stuff on it."

I look over at her sandwich. "I told them no mayonnaise or anything."

"There's lettuce and tomato."

"Oh, sorry. You usually get lettuce and tomato, don't you?"

"Oh, it doesn't matter," she said, shaking her head. "I'll eat it later." Then I remembered that she stopped eating lettuce because of her teeth.

"What have you been doing today?" she asked.

"Oh, just the usual. I took two referrals this morning, both of them four-year-old boys who were throwing chairs in their preschool classrooms. One of them hit the teacher and left a nasty bruise."

"My god! Why do they do that?"

"They have their reasons," I say. "Each one is different. Just like everybody else. We all have reasons for the things we do."

She looks defiant. "I just do whatever I want. I don't give a damn what anybody thinks."

"Yeah, but did you ever wonder why you choose to do those particular things? What makes people want to do anything at all? Why get a perm or listen to music or go to school? What's really at the bottom of it?"

She looked thoughtful. "I'm going to school next semester at J.C. Taking art. Why do I want to do that? I don't know. To feel better about myself, maybe?" She takes a sip of her drink and bites a potato chip, holding it daintily between her thumb and forefinger, as if she'd rather not touch it. "It might make me feel better about who I am. Enhance my self-esteem, like the counselor says. I guess that's why I do things."

After a moment she said, "I've decided to clean things out. I've got some of Donovan's stuff for you to give Tim, if he wants it."

I was surprised. "Sure. What kind of stuff?"

"Oh, some of his school papers and an old yearbook and some notes and poems he wrote." She nodded toward a stack of notebooks on the floor and I recognized a long brown paper towel covered in microscopic handwriting. It was a letter he'd written to an ex-girlfriend back when he was living with me, but never mailed it. I'd noticed it in his room during the months he lived with us. Before he'd gone to live with Tim in Alaska.

"It's been long enough that I'm ready to get rid of some of this stuff. Do you think that's wrong?"

I could not imagine giving away the personal effects of a son who had committed suicide. I said, "No. I think you should do whatever feels right to you. I don't think there is a right and wrong." I prayed to a god I didn't believe in, that I would never have to face anything like that and reminded myself that I don't know how I would act three years later.

"I'm keeping his driver's license and ID card, and the necklace he was wearing. I have his picture and some of his ashes. They're still there on the bookcase." She nodded toward the orange Tupperware container on the second shelf next to his glasses, then tried to take a bite of her sandwich. She pulled it out of her mouth. "God, this is hard." She tapped the chicken with one maroon fingernail making a clicking sound.

I took a bite of potato salad and nodded.

She pulled the bread back and looked at it. "You should call them about this. You should get your money back."

"Think so?" I asked.

"You should. People shouldn't be able to get away with this."

I shrugged my shoulders. "How's the other half?"

She lifted the bun and pushed on the meat with a long red fingernail. "The same. When I was a waitress, I wouldn't have worked at a place that served food like this. You know who gets yelled at when the food's no good? The waitress, that's who. The waitress, who didn't prepare it and has no control over it and is gonna lose her tip, for sure. And then she's supposed to be nice to the customers no matter what assholes they are. I've been down that road more than a few times."

"Gee, I'm sorry, Debby. Would you like some of my salad?"

"No, no."

I remembered again about her teeth.

After taking a sip of her drink she broke off a piece of chicken. "Here, the center seems a little better."

"Good. I hope some of it's edible."

"Yeah, I think I can eat this." She took a bite and leaned her head to the right as if holding a phone to her ear. As she chewed, she adjusted her jaw. "How do you like my new blouse?" She held her elbows akimbo and her white artist's smock billowed out on both sides. "My sister gave it to me for my thirty-ninth birthday. Cost twenty-five bucks."

"Wow," I said. "Twenty-five dollars? Where did she get it?"

"Dillard's. It was on sale."

"Nice."

She stood up and turned around, holding her arms out. "I'm going to wear it to see Dr. Bradford tomorrow. I have to go in for a med check."

"How's that going? Do they have everything regulated yet?"

"Well, I'm on fourteen pills a day now. I take Tegretol twice a day and something for arthritis. Then I've got pills and for nausea and vitamins, I can't even remember all the different names. And I still have to take four sleeping pills every night before I go to bed. It's been years since I could sleep without taking something. When Donovan was little and I was working three jobs I once stayed up for four days. Ended up in the loony bin that time."

"It must be awful." I looked at her and shook my head.

"It is. I just go faster and faster till I spin into outer space. The only way to stop it is to take drugs. Even with them I can't concentrate on anything for more than five minutes. I can't read a book or hold down a job." She shook her head.

"Do conditions like that run in your family?"

"Donovan was like me. A few times we stayed up for two days and nights. I could see myself in him." She beamed with pride. "He was such a good boy, the man of the house. Sometimes when he was in elementary school, I had to call the school to ask him where he'd put something I couldn't find. He always remembered."

"How about your mother?"

"I was adopted, remember? When I was five my foster mother packed me up every weekend and sent me off to visit people who might want to keep me. It was a year before anybody was interested."

I remembered I'd heard this before but still felt stunned at the careless cruelty she had endured. I shook my head and looked down at my salad, ashamed that I was still hungry.

"And I'll tell you, that does something to your self-esteem."

Her comment was so heart wrenching and understated that I laughed. "To put it mildly. Have you ever thought about finding your birth mother?"

"Nope. She lives right here and she's never tried to find me so I'll never look for her. Fuck her. When Donovan was born, they tried to get me to put him up for adoption. But I wouldn't. No way in hell I'd put my kid through what I went through. That's why I say fuck my birth mom."

"Well," I say, "I can see why you'd feel that way."

"Nobody gets beyond the walls I put up. Nobody." She looked at me seriously. "You're as close as I let anybody come. I don't talk about Donovan to anybody but you."

Knowing how little she said to me I understood in a very small way something about the impenetrable barrier she'd placed between herself and the world. I finished my salad and checked my watch. "Oh, look. It's time for me to get back to the office. Seems like I just got here."

"Do you have to? Already?"

"Yeah. I've got a meeting at 1:30."

After she handed me the stack of Donovan's belongings, I hugged her goodbye and headed for the car. When I reached it I looked back, and just before closing the door, she smiled cheerfully and called out, "You know why people do the things they do? It's not self-esteem. It's pain. Avoiding pain."

~

Four years after Donovan's death, Debby was found lying on her couch, dead from a drug overdose. She had been there for several days.

In the years that followed I often thought of both of them … how difficult their time on this earth had been and how hard they'd both worked to succeed in life. I reflected on the potential they'd been born with and how it seemed to have been cruelly shredded away from each of them, a little at a time.

~

A year or so after Debby's death I was looking through an old guitar handbook of Tim's that had once belonged to Donovan and found a note on a brown paper towel. I recognized Donovan's microscopic handwriting and sat down on the sofa to read it.

"I never knew my father but if I had, I'd wish he was like you. Though you may not be able to tell, you've influenced me a lot and a lot of times I think of you when it comes to doing 'the right thing.' Your family is lucky and I am lucky to have you and yours in my life. Thank you."

"Takes me a while to get it, but once I get it, I got it."

His signature was a treble clef.

I still wonder today if Debby's overdose was accidental.

Susan Adger, M.Ed., is a former social worker and web designer, and is a fifth generation Floridian. Her books, *Seashells, Gator Bones, and the Church of Everlasting Liability, and also Moonshine, Mushrooms, and a Boat Named Helen, are both* set in 1930s Florida and were inspired by stories told by her grandmother. She also co-wrote the memoir *A Quiet Voice* about Vietnam veteran Eugene Hairston and his struggle to overcome addiction, post-traumatic stress disorder, and homelessness. She currently resides in Dunedin, Florida near her three children.

DWG

SHIRA PACULT

This Is My Smile

I am Tyr Salinas, reporting for my podcast, *Live Girl,* here in Indian Rocks, Florida. This is a story about my super hard-working friend, Jennifer. She owns the best coffee and wine bar in the entire state called *The Cheshire Cat* in Dunedin.

She graduated from University of Tampa which, in case you didn't know, is a school of very rich kids. After she graduated in art therapy, she went to visit her grandparents.

"Why don't you open your own business and work for yourself?" said Peepaw, which was what she called her grandfather.

Jennifer said with her normal eye twitch and grimace, "What would I do since I don't know how to smile?"

Jennifer lived in her head, so she tried to recall how others expected her to act. On the outside she looked like a normal 26-year-old with brown hair brushed into a ponytail, but on the inside, she dreamed away, keeping her thoughts in a place that often didn't involve anyone else. In there the images kept her busy and she had to remember that others wondered what she imagined. Her grandpa brought her back into the world as she heard him say:

"Well, that's why I am suggesting it, honey. You would not offend your boss." He laughed at his own joke.

Meemaw looked up from her cell phone and stopped looking at the Marco Polo. This ap kept the family connected, showed a video message, with a laughing Arianna, her other nearly engaged granddaughter, with her

"Maybe it would be better if you looked into the CIA and went into some kind of intelligence gathering where no one could figure out what you were really thinking since they would always think you thought the same things."

Jennifer thought for a minute, "I do like secrets, but I don't know any other languages but English."

Peepaw and Jennifer looked down at the tiny Meemaw. Her size-five feet could not touch the floor as she sat on the cushion of her armchair. If it weren't for her white top with rhinestones, she would be lost in the largeness of their 3000 sq. foot living room with its bold red and green accents.

"That would require a lot of desk time," continued Meemaw, "But you'd be by yourself."

Peepaw continued, "Are you good with technology and, more importantly, do you like the idea of being glued to a computer screen all day?"

Jennifer's response was to go into the kitchen and fix her grandparents one of her signature specialties called *Red, White and Blue, So Completely True to You.* She always named her drinks which she would feature on the blackboard at the entrance of the kitchen. It was used as a family bulletin board but when Jennifer visited; her specialty drinks would be written out, themed to the time of year.

On the day of the hatching of the Big Idea, the moment her business gained traction, she served a drink featuring blueberry syrup, maraschino cherries, and cold cream.

As a final touch, the top of the drink was lightly covered with red and blue sprinkles. Sticking out of the top of the dense whipped cream were tiny American flags.

When Meemaw saw her drink being served, she looked up and turned her phone off completely. Jennifer had used handblown glasses from West Virginia with their 4th of July theme featuring stamp-sized images of the signing of the Declaration of Independence.

Meemaw took a deep sip of the holiday brew.

"Honey, this is delicious."

Unfortunately, as was often the case with Meemaw's enjoyment of coffee, some spilled on her shirt. It had been perfectly ironed to lie as an even cover over 36 double D breasts.

As she juggled her way out of her seat, she said with deep concern to Peepaw, "Not again," as she once again had droplets of liquid on her abundant assets.

Peepaw looked lasciviously at his wife of over 55 years. With his blue cloth napkin with white stars designed to look like part of the American flag, he wiped the foam off his moustache.

He watched tiny Meemaw's feet finally hit the floor from her cushioned seat way too high for her. It took an eternity, though, but continuing with determination, she moved to the coffee bar. This feature of the kitchen had been built specifically for Jennifer. She had loved coffee beans ever since she was a kid—smelling them, sorting them, counting them, grinding them, and brewing them for her family.

Jennifer stepped out of the way from cleaning the expresso machine as Meemaw removed a tiny packet of aluminum foil that said, *Removes any coffee stains ASAP.* She dabbed the one-inch cloth over her shirt and the coffee stain disappeared.

"This is so helpful, and it works. It's a Fort Wayne company too. We need to invest in it." She said this every time she had coffee, which was daily and every time she had a spill which was daily, also. Fort Wayne had been their hometown and even though far away now in Florida anything from back home remained a source of pride.

Peepaw stood up which took an eternity to unfurl his 6'11" frame. He picked up Meemaw, all 4'11" of her, all 86 pounds of her, brought her lips to his, and pressed those beautiful bosoms to his chest.

"Honey," he said with gusto, "I did buy the company because I love to watch you wipe those coffee stains off your chest every day."

Meemaw glanced around and whispered into her husband's ear. "Shame on you, Denny, not in front of the kids."

But it didn't matter, since Jennifer engrossed in her cleaning, with furrowed brow, lips tightly pulled over her teeth, continued doing the dishes and had missed the interchange between her grandparents.

After the place sparkled and needed no help, the maid came in to clean the perfectly spotless, marbled top kitchen.

She had been dusting and eavesdropping in the living room during the conversation.

As was the custom in the Ger family, she wore a uniform that matched whatever major holiday was going on. Today, she wore a Betsy Ross costume featuring a white bonnet, a pair of navy pants, a white blousy top with cross straps across the front, and a red jacket. Her shoes were a black patent leather and looked quite comfortable. The landscape crew, domestic help, and office staff also wore their costumes. Workers wore their regular street clothes to the property, but men and women's locker rooms had been installed, all with their outfits sitting tidily in their lockers matched to their sizes. Emboldened by her uniform and in a moment of loyalty and patriotism, the housekeeper, who had taken classes in assertiveness training, said, "Jennifer should open a coffee shop. I mean basically she's been operating yours since she was four."

As if in a moment of divine intervention, the words hanging like the diamonds gleaming in the air caught the attention of the others. Peepaw and Meemaw sat right back down and said in unison, "Jennifer, a star is born."

Jennifer looked up from the glistening machine and went over to her grandfather. "That's me, Peepaw, that's what I want to do."

So, that is how Jennifer came to open the best wine and coffee shop in Dunedin. She painted the walls of her little restaurant to look like the scenes of a café in Italy, and out in her kitchen she begrudgingly fixed the best panini in the world, but only if asked.

Customers came in non-stop to enjoy her holiday drinks. She served them every day of the year, themed to the month. Valentine's Day is my favorite with drinks like Marry Me, French Kiss, and Spice it Up with Sex (pumpkin pie flavors, caramel syrup, coconut milk and cinnamon with her specialty beans.)

Even though you'll never see a grin, the expression on her face shows up as a smile in the taste of her coffee, the comfortable chairs, the books, and the artwork on the wall. You can hear her now familiar greeting "Hello guys" when someone enters. She says it with a straightforward look at her customers, a quick quiver in her eye, and give away prices. As she wipes crumbs of oatmeal cookies off her counter, she catches her reflection in the shining wood and says to herself, "This is my smile."

Shira's poem about the pandemic was published in Ivy Tech's *Ink Cloud*. She wrote a column on home improvement and had feature stories in Fort Wayne's *Journal Gazette*. She blogged on entertainment for vistfortwayne.com. After graduating from Cal Berkeley, she worked in the financial industry. She has four grown children and is also a grandma.

DWG

JOYCE A. STOTTS

Penny-A-Bale

Hilliard Farm, Leavenworth County, Kansas
August 1961

The summer morning dawned slightly cooler than the sweltering day before. The smell of coffee and bacon wafted up the stairs, instantly yanking me wide awake and hungry. Quickly pulling on jeans and one of my dad's old long-sleeved shirts, I was ready for my first day in the hay field. I was glad it was a little cooler, since the haying required something to cover arms and legs for protection from sun, wind, dust, chaff, hay stubble and bugs. I was getting hot already.

The boys came into the kitchen to get me at 7:30 just as I was finishing the last of my pancakes, and we were off to the big hay field, dotted with square bales in haphazard rows. "Here's the deal," my eighteen-year-old brother, Bill announced. "I'm gonna pay you a penny a bale for doing the driving. All you have to do is steer and not run over anybody. We'll throw bales while you're moving along the rows. Drive on the flats as much as possible. We don't want to turn the truck over. Got it?" I nodded but felt no confidence in the task at hand.

A smallish 13-year-old, I didn't know how to drive. Dad sometimes let me steer the tractor or '49 Cadillac while perched on his lap, so I sort of knew how to do that. My feet couldn't reach the brake or clutch from the truck seat anyway, so steering was definitely all I could do.

"What if the truck goes too fast?" I worried aloud.

"It can't," Bill said impatiently. "It'll be locked in first gear. Now, don't worry, we'll be right behind, throwing and stacking as we go. Holler if you need me. Don't be a scaredy cat." I half-heartedly nodded in agreement, still not sure I wanted to be there doing this. I was somewhat encouraged just knowing that my big brother had been haying for a couple of summers, and had turned this into a little business, doing it for the farm neighbors too. His buddies were his haying crew.

Thick black acrid smoke belched out as Bill started the old truck up. The truck protested with some loud hiccupping and popping, which died down after a few minutes to a deep rumble. He let out the clutch in first gear. The truck slowly rolled off. He got out and stood on the running board while I slid across the huge red seat, shiny and worn from wear. He gave a couple of turns of the steering wheel, and told me to do the same, so I could see how hard it was to actually turn it. No power steering on this old machine. Then I was on my own.

I followed the outer row of bales on the edge of the field as Bill had instructed. He and his crew began throwing the bales up onto the flat bed. They laughed, joked and whistled to get each other's attention. All seemed to be going well until I got to the far end and had to turn at a sharp right angle to go along the top of the field. I hollered as loud as I could, and saw Bill running up alongside the cab. He yanked on the stiff steering wheel and said, "Start turning sooner next time, in a big wide circle."

The top of the field was also the ridge of a hill, and now the hot August wind blasted straight through the open cab windows. Along with the wind came dust, hay chaff and bugs each time one of the boys slung a bale up and flopped it on the flat bed. This stung my eyes and made me sneeze. After a good bit of coughing, I learned to hold my breath and breathe only between bales. Sweating, eyes watering, I was soon covered with dust which stuck to the sweat. I could feel a thick mask-like layer caked on my nose whenever I rubbed it after a sneeze. The grasshoppers hopped in and flew out at will, clinging to my shirt sleeves till they got their bearings.

Following the line of bales became harder in the middle of the field, since they weren't really in a line. The truck began to lean to the left downhill side. I quickly turned back up the hill and ran right over a bale, ruining it, but saved the truck from toppling over. As soon as I turned again at the long side of the field, the wind now blew the dust away from me – blessed relief. I looked forward to coming again to that side of the field. I steered around and around the field in circles in ever smaller spirals.

At mid-day, I was grateful when Bill reached into the cab and turned the key. The truck lurched to a stop. My arms ached, my mouth and throat were parched, and I could feel the grit between my teeth. Concentrating so hard on my job, I hadn't noticed that Mom was coming across the field in the pickup. She brought cold lemonade and sandwiches, which we gratefully wolfed down. Nothing I can recall ever tasted better than that sweet, tart, cold lemonade. We sat on the shady side of the truck and leaned up against the big wheels, careful to sit down slowly and carefully in a rolling twist so as not to be stabbed in the rear by the stiff hay stubble.

We finished up the field in the even hotter afternoon. I rode with the boys up to the barn and watched them throw the bales off the truck and neatly stack them. I ran to the house and brought back more lemonade for everyone. By late afternoon we were all done.

Bill and I rode bareback down to the lake on my horse, Molly Bee, and the other boys followed along behind, joking and laughing – glad that the work was done. We headed Molly right into the lake to cool us down quickly, but Molly didn't much like that, so she wheeled and went right back up the other bank. I tried to hang on but slid off her wet slick back into the muddy water – sort of scary and definitely fun. After that, we just let Molly graze while we swam in the lake and washed off the day's dirt and chaff. Actually, Mom wouldn't let us in the house for supper until we had done this. She didn't want all that grit on her kitchen floor.

Bill paid me the "steering" fee. "We had 277 bales," he said. "So here is two dollars and 77 cents." Handing me the money, he grinned. "Now you pay me a penny for that bale you ran over." He held out his hand and I reluctantly handed over the penny. The $2.76 that I earned for those

276 bales didn't quite seem like enough, for such a long, dirty day's work. But now I wouldn't trade all the money in the world for such a memory.

———◆———

Joyce Stotts grew up in a small town and on a farm in Kansas, earning a BS in Secondary Education from Emporia State University and an MS in Educational Technology from University of Kansas. In public schools she taught English, Writing, History, and Social Studies. In addition to her novel entitled *Condo Rondeau*, she is the author and illustrator of a children's picture book, *Suzette Cric-kette*.

DWG

THOMAS McGANN

My Father Is Dying

We are all dying, I know, but my Father is ninety and closer to that ultimate fate than most.

After succumbing to a case of pneumonia that brought a fever and a rattling cough and that helped cause several falls, his children took him to a local hospital where he was immediately admitted.

The pneumonia took its toll. He was no longer himself. The happy demeanor accompanying snatches of songs and an off-key humming had given way to an occasional unhappy mix of anger, despair and, yes, nastiness. He had even taken a couple of weak swings at the nurses and his doctor.

Dad was dying.

It has been reported by some who have had near-death experiences that the history of our lives flashes before our eyes, or through our minds, as death looms. As we, his children, listened to Dad ramble on about his life it was as though the flash of his life's memories had been slowed to a meandering stroll, as though, somehow, he, or Someone Else, knew that he had time enough to meander. Fitfully his spool of memories unwound the tape of his life, present to past, past to present, the immediate present being represented almost not at all, the most distant past dominating.

He cried a lot, sometimes happy tears…happy, blissfully happy. He cried sometimes with a well-deep sadness that was born, I'm guessing, with the ever-nearing proximity of death, frustration at no longer being in control of his own life, and anger with the situation, he felt, in which he had left us children, those he loved most.

Or maybe his tears sprang from unhappy memories, lost opportunities, disappointments with us children. We were never to know about those lost secrets he was going to take with him. He saved us from that pain.

That coupled with the embarrassment over his physical condition made for some unhappy days. Incontinent bowels, an uncomfortable catheter, a runny nose he had to struggle to wipe with shaking hands, teary eyes that left moist, itchy paths as they slowly eroded the parched, gray-stubbled cheeks—wiping tears and a runny nose with that same crumbled, fraying tissue.

Worse than the periodic crying spells were the fierce bouts of anger that had him stiffen, bend his arms at the elbows, lift them off his chest as his body shook with fury and frustration.

He would speak of this as his life unraveled into my ears, his visions past, present, but…unfinished, interrupted, half-forgotten in the misty memory's fields of dreams.

I love him so.

Watching him go…

Listening…

Sometimes I feed him.

Sometimes he feeds himself, slowly, awkwardly, food trembled off the spoon.

Often, we sit in silence.

Then his ramblings will begin.

Rambling…on
        and on…
                and on.

As I listen…

    between the words

For ideas

Missed or missing

I listen

For wisdom from my dying Father.

Who is now dead.

———————◆———————

Thomas McGann is a native Long Islander, a graduate of Bishop Loughlin MHS and the U.S. Coast Guard Academy. Beside a military career that included a tour in Viet Nam, Tom has been involved in several businesses on Long Island, NY. In addition, Tom spent years digging clams and painting houses. His passion is writing. He wrote a political column for the online magazine examiner.com and is a contributor to the *Fire Island News* and has collected these articles in

Historical Anecdotes. He is also the author of the young adult fantasy, *The Riddle of Riddles*, the motorcycle thriller, *Chance*, several plays, numerous short stories and essays, and reams of poetry. Sailing, motorcycling, and reading are his hobbies, but family is his life. He maintains two websites: thomasmcgann.com & theriddleofriddles.com.

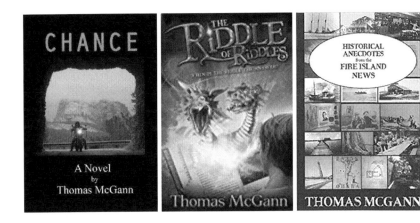

Buy Tom's books on Amazon. Copyright 2021. All rights reserved.

DWG

DAVID A. FOOTE

Couth

A True Story, 1975

In pursuit of owning an automobile dealership, there are several steps one must complete successfully before a manufacturer will consider you as a dealer/principle. The first step is to prove oneself on a salesroom floor with good gross margins over several years. Then you must move into sales management where the ability to work with others is measured in vehicles sold, customer satisfaction, and, most importantly, with high profit margins. The third step is becoming a general manager.

I had completed the first parts of my learning curve as a salesperson for a Pontiac dealer and then as a sales manager in a Ford store; both were successes that led to my being hired as a general manager by Les MacDonald, who had just acquired a large Toronto dealership named Mainway Ford. It was located in the east end of the city in a building erected in the early 20's.

What neither Les nor I didn't know was that the previous owner had put a "for-sale" sign on the business a full year before it sold. Good employees had fled. The not-so-good stayed and helped themselves to freebies wherever they could. Pilfering and conniving were everywhere.

After Les took the keys and the dealership was officially under new ownership, the first order of business was to review the various departments to see where changes were needed. This shake-up occurred mostly at the management level, with mechanics, sales staff, and parts people keeping their jobs. The hunt for managers was on.

I'm now knowledgeable on how a car dealership and the various departments work, but at the time I was not a bona-fide expert on each of the areas, so I sought out and hired the best in service, body shop, leasing and sales management personnel.

An integral part of any business is the administrative office where the necessary paperwork for payroll and accounts payable and receivable must be recorded and handled accurately and efficiently along with the myriad of items from workmen's comp to income taxes.

One area indicative of a dealership's financial health is the amount and the age of its accounts-receivable list. Those are the monies owed to the company by various vendors from body shops to other repair garages and whoever else buys parts or services and is allowed to pay in 30 days.

The amount is often high. It wouldn't be unusual for three hundred thousand dollars to be floating around out there. This credit system works well if the accounts are paid in full within the 30-days.

Most are, but some aren't.

The next part is debt aging—how much is within the 30 days, how much is over but yet under 90, and how much is over that but still under 180 days.

After that, the account usually goes to a collection agency.

For Mainway, I expected to find this account in total disarray with a lot of money well over the 90 and the 180-day marks. But I was nicely surprised when I found that most of the accounts were being paid within the 30-day time frame. Few went over it, and none hit the 90-day mark.

I was impressed until I found out why. The woman who looked after the receivable account was a terror on the phone. A hapless vendor who was approaching the 30-day limit would get a call from this woman (I'll call her Maude) who would have made Attila-the-Hun sound meek and mild.

She used the "F" word in almost every sentence with threats that the mafia would come looking if payment wasn't made on time. God forbid anyone went over the 30 days. Plus, she had the home phone numbers for all and wouldn't hesitate to make calls at midnight for the monies to be brought in. Mainway had the cleanest accounts-receivable file that I have ever seen.

That was the upside.

The downside, besides filling the office air with her barroom-brawl of "get-the-money-in-TODAY-or-ELSE" dialogue, Maude, in her late 20's, had no idea what "office decorum" was all about. She dressed in tight-fitting jeans with holes in all the inappropriate places and that hadn't seen a washing machine in ages. It was the same for her braless T shirts. Make-up wasn't her thing, nor was washing her hair. Like her clothes, from one month to the next, it didn't get washed.

She had to go.

But firing a person from one of the dealership's many departments is not the general manager's job. When someone is hired to take on this task (in this case Bob Burnham to run the accounting department), "the person responsible for getting the job done must also have the corresponding authority to change and do whatever is necessary so that success is achieved." Bob agreed that he had to fire Maude.

In business, most managers can handle the upside of the day-to-day routines. But one of the downsides is letting someone go. Bob was no exception in his fear of meeting employees face-to-face and telling them they're being terminated. In Maude's case, he waffled on performing the task. Every time I asked him *when*, he said "tomorrow."

Tomorrow finally came.

He called her into his office and closed the door, a sure sign something bad was about to happen. In his recollection to me of what transpired, he said that he started nervously with the typical words of, "Maude, I don't have good news, I have to let you go."

An employee's immediate response is usually, "Why?"

And this time Maude followed up by, "Oh gosh, Mr. Burnham, you can't let me go. I need this job so bad."

Burnham's underpinning, while at the best of times not all that strong, started to weaken. He blurted out, "I'm sorry, Maude. It's just that there are a whole bunch of reasons as to why."

She leaned towards him and asked, "Well, tell me of one of them."

"Your arithmetic is atrocious. The other girls are always making corrections for you."

Maude thought a minute.

"Yes, I understand I'm not that good at counting up numbers. What I can do is my boyfriend is real good at math. I can get him to teach me, so I'll be much better at arithmetic."

Getting exasperated, Bob countered with, "Well, if it was just the math, we wouldn't be sitting here."

"What else?" Maude asked.

"It's what you wear to the office that just doesn't work. You're always in tattered jeans and a tight T shirt with no bra that has the salesmen invading the office with the phoniest of excuses just to look at your boobs."

Silence invaded the room.

"Mr. Burnham, you are right. I don't have much of a wardrobe because I don't know how to buy clothes that fit."

"Or have seen a washing machine," Bob added.

"You're right. You're perfectly right. What I can do is have Dorothy help me. She is always nicely dressed. I'll have her take me out and buy a whole new wardrobe that will make you proud of me. And I'll get my landlord to show me how to operate the building's washing machine and dryer. What else can I do?"

"Maude, this is going nowhere," said Bob. "You can do all of what I have mentioned, but **good** gosh, woman, it seems that you never wash your hair or face for that matter. I've never seen you wearing makeup."

Again, Maude paused. "You are right again, Mr. Burnham. Judy, the night switchboard girl, you know the one with the monster tits?"

Bob glanced upwards. "Yes, I know who you mean."

"She is always done up so nice. I'll get her to teach me how to use make-up, and I'll start going to her hairdresser, so I can learn how to keep my hair neat and clean."

Then she added, "Is there anything else?"

Bob was now flustered. For every reason he gave her as to why he had to let her go, she countered with a good reason why she shouldn't be.

In desperation, he blurted, "It's because you lack couth."

Maude sat back, scratched her forehead, started to speak, stopped, went deep into thought, looked up at Bob, and finally spoke.

"What the fuck is *couth*?"

She got fired.

David is a longtime participant in the Dunedin Writers Group, spending his winters here. His summer home is in Skerryvore, Ontario, where he writes a column for a chain of newspapers called Metroland Media. He has had a long and successful career in the automotive field, and is the author of a memoir *Footprints in Skerryvore* and a suspense thriller, *I Didn't Kill the Third Girl.*

DWG

RHONDA RINEKER

The Tractor Kerfuffle

It was summertime and things on the farm needed doing. And I was just the person to get them done, by golly. Fences, ditches, feed troughs, paddocks, the barn, gravel roads, pastures—you name it, it was on my list. We had five hundred acres and one farm hand, Steve. He was in his mid-twenties, just a few years younger than I. Tall, lanky, he sported a shaggy beard, chewed tobacco, and was not known to be a hard worker. He preferred a little work in the morning and a shade tree in the afternoon. I decided to bring up the subject to my husband at breakfast.

"Bud," I said as I watched him munch his toast, "I've been thinking. I'd like to work around the farm this summer, take a break from the shops. I'll come in when you need me."

Bud chuckled. "I'll see what I can do, move some people around, but it should be okay. I feel sorry for Steve, though. I know you're going to work his butt off."

"Yeah, no way he'll let a girl outwork him, male ego and all. He'll play right into my hands." I smiled.

A week later we had everything arranged. Steve and I had a long list of things to do. I liked outside, physical work and couldn't wait to get started.

"Okay, Steve," I said, "what should we do first?"

"Well," he answered, "I figure we can work on the feed troughs up on the hill. I loaded the stuff in back of the truck. You better grab another hammer. You know how to use a hammer, don't you?"

"Oh, har-har, very funny. Stop by the barn and I'll grab one."

I climbed into his old truck.

We worked until early afternoon. It was getting pretty hot, so we decided to get a sandwich at the little store in town. Town consisted of one gas station, two bars—The Possum Trott Inn and The Etonian—as well as Dyers General Store and Boston Food Mart, which was where we bought our lunch. They made the sandwiches fresh, threw in a bag of chips and a drink. The prices were pretty cheap, so it was a popular place for lunch. We grabbed our goodies, went back to the truck. Windows down, we sat in the cab and started to eat. A bunch of farmers in coveralls sauntered by.

The smell made its way on the hot summer breeze and through our open windows.

"Man, they stink," Steve said. "Good thing we got here first."

"What *is* that smell?" I asked.

"Pig farmers."

"Let's hit the road before they come back out."

~

Every day, we worked down our list—feed troughs repaired, barn cleaned, paddocks weeded, hay stacked in the barn loft, and gravel road graded. I felt good with our progress. Steve was clearing the fence rows and I was clearing out the drainage ditches. We were well into our third week of work.

The next morning at breakfast, Bud grinned as he watched me eat my pop tart.

"What's so funny?" I mumbled with my mouth full.

"Steve asked me when you're going back full time at the shop. I asked why, and he said he just wondered. I figure you're working him too hard."

"Well, he'll have an easy day today. We're going to mow the fields. So, he'll get to ride on the tractor the whole time. You know how much he likes that."

"Yeah, and so do you."

"That's true, it is fun."

"You both be careful."

~

I met Steve at the barn where we filled the two tractors with diesel fuel from our tank. I lovingly looked at the big red, dual-wheel Allis Chalmers tractor and the fifteen-foot bat-wing bushhog. The bushhog had three rotary blades that could cut through most anything and folded up when not in use.

"I'll take the big tractor," Steve said as he got up onto the seat, "with the batwing bush hog, and mow the back pasture. You can take the other tractor and bush hog and mow the middle one."

"Hey, why do you get to use the big tractor!"

"Have you ever drove the big tractor and used the big bush hog?" he demanded as he looked down at me.

"Uh, … no," I mumbled.

"Well, I guess that's why, then."

"All right," I replied and stomped over to the Kubota. "I'll need your help to hook up the bush hog."

"Okay, go on over there, back the tractor up to it and I'll meet you there."

All hooked up, we proceeded to our assigned pastures. A couple of hours into mowing, I see Steve, all muddy, striding across the field toward me. I took the tractor out of gear, idled it down, and waited for him to reach me. I looked him over, muddy from head to toe. I couldn't help but laugh.

"What's the matter?" I yell, above the noise of the motor. "Fall off the tractor?"

"No, I didn't fall off the tractor. I got stuck and need you to come back there and pull me out."

"How'd you get stuck?"

"Well, if you haf'ta know, I was mowin' around the pond and … well, I got stuck in the slew."

"Stuck in the slew? How'd you do that?"

He took a big breath, looked down at his mud-covered boots. "Can we just go pull it out?"

I turned off the tractor. We unhooked the mower. He hopped on the fender and we rode back to the barn to find a chain. Then, it was a quiet ride to the back field. But he must have felt me giggling inside.

"It's not funny," he said, scowling.

"No … but it kinda is."

"Back the tractor up until I tell you to stop," he instructed me.

I slowly did so.

"Stop!" he barked.

Then he hooked the chain up to both tractors.

"Okay," he said. "Now, when I tell you, just ease the tractor up slowly until the chain is tight, and then go forward real slow. I'll tell you when to give it gas."

I put the tractor into gear, slowly let out the clutch.

"Go!" Steve hollered.

The chain tightened, the tractor moved forward, and the wheels started to spin, digging deep into the mud. Mud flew everywhere.

"Stop! Stop!" Steve yelled.

I turned the tractor off, jumped down and looked at him.

"I thought you knew what you were doing!" I shouted. "Now, looked what happened. Both tractors are stuck!"

"Let's go get the little Ford," he replied, "and see if we can pull out yours."

He turned and headed toward the barn.

"What a stupid idiot," I mumbled as I hiked behind him.

We rode our third tractor, a small blue Ford, to the back pasture and hooked it to the second tractor.

"I'll do it this time," Steve grumbled, giving me a dirty look like it was my fault that he's an idiot.

He slowly put the tractor in gear, pulling the chain tight. I watched the wheels sinking into the mud and dove out of the way as the gump began to fly. Damn if he didn't get that one stuck—three for three.

I won't tell you the word he used! He took off his cap and rubbed his head.

"Let's see if Dolly's around, maybe he can get them out."

We walked back to the barn, jumped in Steve's truck and went in search of help. But, Dolly, our neighbor's farmhand and Steve's pal, was nowhere to be found. We drove up and down the road, not a living soul around. Heads hung and feeling dejected, we headed back to our farm.

"We have to get these tractors pulled out before Bud gets home," I moaned. "He's gonna think we're both idiots. I'll never hear the end of it!"

"Only one thing left to try," Steve said as we bounced down the road to the collection of tractors in the back pasture.

"What are you going to do!" I asked.

He reversed up to the little Ford, got out and hooked the chain to the truck. I strolled over and stood in the shade. I did not have a good feeling—after all, the truck was old and two-wheel drive.

"Damn!" I muttered to the ragweed.

Well, you guessed it.

We both stared. Now, three tractors and a truck! A convoy of disaster. We both turned and trod to the house. Time to settle on that bench under the big oak tree. I brought out two iced teas, and not saying a word, we waited for Bud to come home. It wouldn't be long, since we spent most of the day trying to get our equipment unstuck. Not much mowing got done.

"This is so embarrassing," I finally muttered.

"Yep," Steve answered. He took a sip of his tea and leaned back.

"What do you think Bud's gonna say?" I asked, pacing, too nervous to sit.

"Looks like we gonna find out," Steve answered. "He just pulled in the drive."

Bud parked and strolled over.

"I'm glad some of us can lounge around all day in the shade," he joked. Then he saw our expressions. "Okay, what's wrong? Why the funny looks on your faces?"

"Uh ..." I started. "Well, uh, see, Bud, we kinda got the tractor stuck in the mud. You think you can use your four-wheel drive truck to pull it out?"

"Stuck, huh?" Bud said. "Sure thing, get in the truck and we'll take a look."

When we piled in the cab, Bud looked over at Steve.

"Why didn't you just pull it out with the other tractor?"

I looked out the side window. Steve rubbed his beard and said, "You'll see."

We drove through the little stand of trees to the back pasture. And there they were, in all their glory—three tractors and the old green truck in a nice, neat row.

"Jeez!" Bud exclaimed. "You have got to be kidding me!"

He got out of the truck and slammed the door. We could hear him cussing as we sat in the cab staring out the windshield. He stomped over to the tractors.

"Steve!" he yelled. "Back my truck over here. "We'll get your piece of crap truck out first. Make sure you put mine in four-wheel drive. I'll tell you when to start pulling."

Bud unhooked the chain from the back of Steve's truck and hooked it to the front axle and the tow bar of the four-wheel drive.

"Get in Steve's truck," he yelled at me, "and keep the wheel straight."

And damn, if it didn't work. We followed this procedure with the tractors, too. Once we had the tractors freed up, we connected the mowers and drove them to the barn. Then we hiked back for the two trucks—I figured I'd better go along. We didn't say a word. That march seemed to take forever. When we finally got to the two trucks, we just kinda stood there, not knowing quite what to say.

Well, Steve looks at me and I look at Bud, and we all kinda looked at each other, and Steve started to say something but before he could, Bud held up his and … there was what I guess is called a pregnant pause until Bud says, "I don't wanna to know," … and we all burst out laughing.

New to writing, Rhonda S. Rineker is focused on autobiography. She was born and raised in Virginia and now lives in Dunedin. She is a business owner. With her permission, this piece was mentored by Jon Michael Miller.

DWG

KEVIN E. CORRIGAN

The Third Vote

Anyone familiar with my grandfather, Theodore, knew he didn't always practice what some folks thought he was preaching. For example, if he were a true Socialist, why then did he put the house his recently married daughter and son-in-law were living in with his newborn grandchild, on the market? Ma and Pa weren't looking for a handout, they just needed some time to build the new house in Henrietta, NY. where my sibs and I would ultimately be raised. After working an 8-to-5 job as a carpenter at Sears and Roebuck on Monroe Avenue in Rochester, dad would then drive to the lot and work on the house well into the night.

The O'Neill's, who lived next door, kindly let dad use their electricity so he could run flood lights that allowed he and my uncle to work long after dark. But even at this level, two skilled craftsmen would have a difficult time getting the house closed in before the first snow. Maybe grandpa thought he was doing my parents a favor by providing more of an incentive when he informed them that they needed to be out by a certain date. But this *sink or swim* mentality sounded more like a dyed-in-the-wool capitalist than a socialist to me.

And who cares if mom was his only daughter? Once you start making exceptions to the rules, there's just no telling where it may end. So, while she was nursing one baby with another on the way, grandpa was determined not to have my parents on *his* nipple any longer.

It was a conundrum! If grandpa truly believed that the proletariat class was being exploited, why then did he refuse to drive grandma to her waitressing job in the city? All she wanted was bring in a little extra income. Did her insistence on being the least bit independent threaten him that much? Well… since grandma had to hitchhike home half the time, perhaps it did! While Ted may have verbally insisted on the benefits of the "Common Collective", his actions seemed to speak otherwise. Considering these… *inconsistencies* let's call them, for Ted to then run for elected office in 1956 as a Socialist might seem to the not-so-casual observer as a bit surprising, *if not hypocritical.*

And what drove Theodore to this dubious decision? Was it the county building inspector who wouldn't pass the inspection on the lake house because it had only one entry door and in Ted's mind, one door is all you need? So what if there was a fire? Why can't you use the same darn door you came in through? Talk about government overreach! Another possibility was that Ted was seriously considering becoming a servant for the public good, (this idea was soon dispelled by folks who knew him). Or was it that the recent McCarthy hearings had gotten his socialist dander up? In any case, once word got out, interest in the election took off like a Roman Commie candle.

Predictably, when it was all over, my grandfather lost. The very idea of someone running as a commie was so abhorrent to area voters that his opponent won in a landslide. Of the eight hundred and twenty-seven votes that were ultimately cast, gramps received three. Yep, three votes! *And who were those three votes?* Well, it was certain Ted voted for himself, so that was one. Grandma probably voted for him too, if only to keep him occupied attending nightly meetings so she could have a little piece and quiet for a change. Although the scuttlebutt was that secretly she had taken some of that hard earned money she made waitressing and gave it to his opponent's campaign.

But who on earth could the third vote be?

It's all the town talked about! Nobody really cared who won (as long as it wasn't Ted). All anyone cared about, all they really wanted to know. was who cast that third vote!

Suspicions were aroused and folks started looking askance at neighbors they'd known most of their lives. The mailman who was seen talking to Ted immediately came under suspicion. Anyone who owned a dog that was known to visit Ted for a nice meaty bone suddenly were thought to be clandestine canine commies.

OMG! It could be someone we know! Someone we trusted! (Or thought we could.)

And what was the result of this Pandemic of Political Paranoia? Backyard BBQs were not being held as frequently. Birthday parties for the kiddies went unattended. The Friday night bridge game where the points of view used to flow as freely as the beer suddenly dried up. Even the Parson Parsimonious of the Non-denominational Anti-sinafying

Defamation Church gave a sermon that "the only good American Commie, was an ex-communicated American Commie." Then someone remind the parson that only the Catholic Church can ex-communicate you to which the good parson replied, "There's all kinds of ex-communication...."

So now, it wasn't so much that grandpa was the focus, nor my grandmother, it was *the person who cast the third vote.* And it didn't seem to matter that the third vote really didn't matter. What mattered was that no one knew who that third vote was. But it was clear that it came from within the community. And if at all possible, that third voter, whoever they (or it) were, should be driven from their midst, if the Parson Parsimonious of the Non-denominational Anti-sinafying Defamation Church had anything to say about it!

The problem was that all this fear, anger and mistrust had begun to have unforeseen consequences. Family get togethers suffered. Friendly neighbors suddenly weren't so friendly or neighborly. And then, along with social gatherings, the collection plate started drying up! So, the good parson, while he didn't recant or apologize, did say at the following Sunday service, that his remarks were taken completely out of context.

Some weeks later, in an effort to allay fears and instill calm, an editorial appeared in the Livonia Gazette which said that, among other things, it "is the character of patriotic Americans to occasionally disagree with one another." To which a local resident replied in the op-ed section the following week that "the editor didn't know what the hell he was talking about!"

After that, birthday parties started being planned, backyard BBQs were being held once again and while people still were a bit cagey about offering their personal points of view at the Friday night bridge game, things sort of got back to normal.

And my grandpa Ted, he went back to tending his garden, giving the neighborhood dogs some treats and complaining about the government, like any good American.

Believing that everyday life offers us plenty of opportunities to laugh, mostly at ourselves, Kevin especially likes to write stories about his experiences from a humorous point of view.

Star2steerby@gmail.com.

DWG

SOL GUMPRICHT

Fruit of the Poisonous Tree
1 The Hash Man

Baltimore, 1968

Leo looked around his new apartment in downtown Baltimore. It was early summer of 1969. He was pleased with the place, and with himself. After all, he'd lost fifty-four pounds in the past five months, let his hair grow out and began growing a beard – things he could never have done while he was the General Sales Manager at Horn Ford in northwest Baltimore.

The apartment was an exquisite two-bedroom, one bath with newly sanded hardwood oak floors, twelve-foot ceilings and a large fireplace in every room but the kitchen and baths. It occupied the entire first floor of the four-story, 150-year-old building. Behind the structure, in what was once a livery stable, sat a beautiful efficiency apartment complete with a kitchenette and a full bathroom.

Yes, Leo loved his new pad and he paid well below market value. The owners, Richard and Cindy Pecora, were both attorneys fresh out of law school and had recently passed the Maryland State Bar Exam. Cindy was pregnant with their first child. Richard's father was a prominent real estate lawyer, and they both joined his law firm. Leo got a kick out of watching "the lovebirds," as he called them. He saw a lot of them because they were his upstairs neighbors. The senior Pecora had given his only son the corner building they resided in, and the adjacent building as a combination wedding-graduation-passing-the-bar present. *Helluva a nice gift,* Leo thought.

He had met Richard a couple of years earlier while the latter was an intern at the law offices of Joseph Jaye Wise, a thirty-seven-year-old defense attorney, and Leo's best friend. As much as Leo loved the new apartment, he knew it represented a tacit recognition that his eight-year affair/marriage to Angela was over. Leo and Angela had lived in a suburban Baltimore flat for seven years. After she and their son, Clifford moved out, Leo stayed an additional six months, hoping they would come back. Leo had named their son after the great jazz trumpet player, Clifford Brown, who died in a car crash while still in his twenties.

Oh, sure, he and Angela had separated several times before, but on each occasion, she took Clifford and moved in with her Aunt Viola. Leo swore on a stack of bibles that he would stop gambling and never make another bet. Angela knew he was an atheist, but he would woo her, silver-tongued devil that he was, and she would always move back in. This time was different, though. This time she went out and got a job. She was a trained nurse and had no problem finding work.

Two weeks later she rented her own apartment. To say his heart was broken would be an understatement. It was shattered! The pain in his soul was excruciating! She was the great love of his life and he had lost her!

Several weeks after moving into the new apartment, the doorbell rang. It was a Saturday morning. He opened the door, and there stood Karl Michael Brandt. He was not alone.

"Hey, Leo," said Karl, "let me introduce you to my good friend Laura."

Leo gave her the onceover. He liked what he saw and spontaneously broke into a song: "Laura, you're the face in the misty light. Footsteps that you hear down the hall." Leo paraphrased the old Johnny Mercer lyrics, but it fell with a thud and a quizzical look on Laura's face.

"It's the opening line of a very famous song and film of the same name from the mid-1940's," Leo explained.

After Laura smiled a beautifully innocent smile. Leo changed the subject.

"I just love the flower in your hair. You must be one of those flower children I've been hearing and reading about, and if, indeed, you are, you're the first one I've ever personally met."

The deep red rose was nestled in her long brown hair, perched just above her left ear. She seemed quite young. *I hope she's at least eighteen*, he thought. She also seemed rather shy, but when he looked into those deep brown, Sephardic eyes, he knew there was something going on.

Karl lived next door to Angela and Clifford His wife Lisa had called Angela to tell her about the "apartment for rent" sign that had just sprung up in the front yard of the house next door. Karl and Lisa had a daughter Leslie, who was also seven and attended the same private school as

Clifford They were good friends, and with Angela working the twelve-to-eight-night shift, this move made a lot of sense.

The past year had been life-changing for Karl, who was a documentary film maker for Guggenheim Films in D.C. He was the producer/cinematographer of a film about then Maryland Governor Spiro T. Agnew. Shortly after completing the biographical documentary, "Tricky Dick" Nixon, as Leo called him, selected Agnew to become his running mate as vice-president. Suddenly, everyone took notice, and Karl went on to win his Pulitzer Prize, and a Peabody Award to boot.

Leo assumed, correctly he later learned, that Karl and Laura had spent the night together. He also assumed, correctly, that Laura was somehow involved with filmmaking or photography.

Karl interrupted Leo's thoughts. "I turned Laura on to some of that Afghani primo hash last night. It blew her mind. She asked if I could get her some, so I told her I would introduce her to The Hash Man."

Leo grinned at Karl then at Laura. "They only call me that because of my famous recipe for corned beef hash."

But he resented Karl's bringing a complete stranger to his place, then talking about committing a felony as if it were nothing more than giving a pal an aspirin. He would hold his anger in, for the moment.

"I've known this guy for over ten years," Karl said to Laura. "When was it, Leo – 1958? The first time you came to my house and brought your trumpet to jam with my quartet? Even then, they called you The Hash Man. Come to think of it, you're the one gave our band its name: 'Keepers of the Sacred Riff'. Later, we shortened it to The Riff Keepers."

"My I use the bathroom?" Laura asked.

He directed her down the hall, second door on the right. She was so polite, maybe coy, but there was definitely something ... what was the word? Leo thought. *Sweet!* Yes, there was something sweet about her. These days, he wasn't used to *sweet*.

As soon as they heard the bathroom door close, Karl said softly, "I need to be getting home. Laura needs a place to crash for a few days, and you being recently singled...."

"How old is she?" Leo asked.

"Nineteen."

"Are you sure?"

"Positive, just completed her second year at U. of Maryland. And last year she applied for an internship at Guggenheim. I mentored her, eighteen then, and a very talented photographer."

"Okay, but I need to hear it from her lips."

"What, that she's nineteen?"

"No, that she wants to crash here. Hell, I'm a total stranger."

"Oh, that's no problem."

"Wow!" Laura said, returning from the bathroom. "That bathtub is huge. I've never seen anything like it."

"Yeah," Leo said, "I had the same reaction the first time I saw it while viewing this place, cast iron. newly re-porcelained when the entire building was refurbished."

"And those bronze lion paws," she added.

"I can tell you're a highly refined young lady. Would you two like some coffee or tea? Water? Beer? Or maybe you'd like to smoke some of that aforementioned hashish?"

Laura looked toward Karl as if he was her guardian.

"Nothing for me," Karl answered. He looked knowingly at Leo. "I gotta be going. But, uh, would it be okay if Laura crashed here for two or three days?"

Leo looked at Laura.

She smiled sheepishly. "I've been fighting with my mother since I told her I'm dropping out of college. It's only for one semester but she freaked out about it. She and my dad are leaving for Europe next week on a two-week vacation, and I need somewhere to stay until they leave. Karl said maybe you'd consider it. He assured me you're cool, and I'm beginning to believe him. Maybe I could just move into that bathtub."

Leo couldn't wipe the smile off his face. "I would be honored to have you grace my humble abode."

"Thanks. You're a life saver." She turned to Karl. "My overnight bag and camera are in your trunk."

"I'll be happy to get it for you, Laura."

"Oh, they're light, but maybe you could prepare the pipe while I get them."

"Ah!" Leo said, surprised at her assertiveness. "I think I might manage that."

A few minutes later she returned, *sans* Karl, but with a small suitcase, a canvas shopping bag and a gleam in her eye.

With her bags on his floor, Leo hesitated to take them to his bedroom – he wasn't about to equal her presumptuousness. But he certainly didn't want to take them to the guest room – completely wrong signal. So holding the long wooden pipe, fully loaded, he gallantly gestured toward the sofa. Seated side by side, he smelled her subtle perfume, her innocent beauty swamping all his senses. He handed her the pipe.

"Now," he managed to say, "this is Afghani primo, number one, the most potent hashish in the world. Pull very slowly and do not take too big a hit, got it? It expands in your lungs and if you inhale too much, you'll start coughing your head off and that would be very wasteful. Ideally, you'll inhale the right amount, so hold it in as long as you can, then exhale very slowly. One hit will get you stoned, two will get you very stoned, three is like tripping on acid. Are you sure you're ready for this? Should I try to talk you out of it?"

"Would you like to?"

"Maybe I should. You're quite young."

"Karl has taken me around the block," she said, grinning, "or might I say, down the primrose path of getting high. I'm into it. Oh, and I happen to dig older men."

"Hey, I'm only twenty-five. Karl's over thirty."

"But you seem much older. Wiser. And very cool, as if you've lived a lot in your twenty-five years. And thank you so much, Professor, for your detailed instructions, but I smoked some with Karl last night. Uh, not in a pipe, though. He mixed it with some tobacco and rolled a joint."

"Yeah, that's how the Europeans do it. Do you smoke cigarettes?"

"Not usually, though I may have one if I'm drinking at a party or after...."

"Or after ... what?"

She smiled, but this smile was anything but innocent. "Oh," she said softly. "I have a feeling you know what."

He lit the pipe with a long wooden match, and she followed his directions precisely. He could see her holding back the urge to cough, and she released a tiny cloud of smoke so as not to start. Then, very slowly, she exhaled. Leo watched as her eyes glazed over, then he began a pull on the pipe himself. Her eyes opened and she gazed at him.

"Oh, my god!" she said, dreamily.

They sat in silence, letting the cannabis do its magic. Soon, she took his hand and leaned over to kiss him, a slow, gentle kiss, during which he placed his hand on one of her ample breasts.

The next few days were full of long, sensual baths by candlelight and incense. Great joy and bliss had returned to his life, just when he needed it most. These were precious moments when Angela was not on his mind. "Surcease from sorrow, sorrow for the lost Lenore," he remembered from Poe's "The Raven," only in this case it was not "Lenore" who was lost. It was Angela.

Laura seemed insatiable, one of her many virtues to Leo. When they did come up for air, he took her to the Green Earth Health Food Store and Juice Bar. He introduced her to raw vegetable juices and ordered her the same drink he had every day – carrot, celery, beet, spinach and ginger root. Because this was her first experience with veggie juices, he suggested the addition of a red delicious apple to sweeten it. He supersized both drinks to twenty ounces and watched her carefully as she took that first sip.

"Interesting," she said. "Yum."

Leo was relieved. Before leaving the store, he walked over to the book section and picked up two. He handed them to her.

"My gift to you," he said. She looked at the titles: *Raw Vegetable Juices (What's Missing in Your Body?)* and *The Mucousless Diet Healing System.* "These two books changed my life," he told her.

When they stepped out onto the street, he pointed to the restaurant next door, The Indian Palace.

"Do you like Indian food, Laura?"

"Never tried it."

"Would you like to?"

"Sure, why not?"

"Okay, dinner tonight."

Back at the apartment they settled into the living room, Leo on his stuffed recliner, Laura stretched out on the sofa in a short dress that exposed her tanned thighs. "So how did you and Karl meet," Leo asked. He already knew the answer, but wanted her perspective.

"Well, last summer," she said, "I applied for an internship at Guggenheim Films. Karl interviewed and hired me. It didn't pay much, but I would have worked for nothing just to learn from him. All I've ever wanted to do was photography, and Karl is one of the world's best. I pinched myself every day, and learned so much from him. Then toward the end of the summer, he invited me to lunch, said he wanted me to meet a friend of his from San Francisco, who, along with some partners, had started a magazine devoted entirely to music, mostly rock and roll – *Rolling Stone*, have you heard of it?"

Leo shook his head, no. "But I don't follow rock and roll."

"Anyway, his name is David and we've kept in touch. A few weeks ago, he called and said the magazine has taken off big time. He told me about some rock concerts that are all within driving distance of Baltimore, this summer, said if I send him pictures, he could pay me a hundred dollars for each one used in the magazine."

"Nice," said Leo. "Congrats."

"Yeah, two of the concerts have already happened, one in Virginia, the other on the Jersey Shore. I went to both and took dozens of pictures. I sent David thirty of the best, and guess what."

"Okay, what?" Leo could sense the excitement swelling up within her.

"He showed them to the big boss and he loved my work. He said they were using seven of them in the next issue. Then three or four days later, I get this manila envelope, special delivery, from San Francisco. My heart pounding, I opened it. And guess what was inside?"

"What?" he asked.

"A letter from David, two checks made out to me, and two plastic press passes with *Rolling Stone Magazine* and my name on them. Both checks were from the magazine."

"Why two?" Leo asked. "Should have been just one for seven bills."

"Yes, that was one of them but it added three hundred for expenses. The second check was for five hundred for a roundtrip airline ticket to San Fran to discuss joining the team as a fulltime staff photographer."

Laura was ecstatic.

"Oh," she added, "and the two press passes were so I wouldn't have to pay for future concerts and, also, to get me access to backstage, one for me and the other for a friend. And, I almost forgot, there were also two flyers for upcoming concerts. The first is this Saturday at Laurel Race Course. Do you know where that is?"

Leo knew all too well where it was. "Yes, I know," was all he said.

"The second concert is a three-day affair in Woodstock, New York. David said this one could be historic with over thirty big name bands and more than a quarter million people expected. *Rolling Stone* is going all out on this one. They've rented an entire motel in Bethel, New York, for a whole week. I would love for you to come with me for both events. How 'bout it?"

Leo was flattered. He'd never been to a rock concert or festival in his life. But being with this phenomenal young woman was the lure. He thought for a moment.

"I'm a definite for Saturday at Laurel. Now, what are the dates of that three-day affair?"

She sat up and pulled both flyers out of the envelope. "August fifteenth, sixteenth and seventeenth."

"I'll have to get back to you on that one," he answered, knowing full well he had already purchased a roundtrip ticket to London, leaving on August tenth for two weeks. But why break the mood? It was presently the end of June.

Leo and Laura were at the India Palace for dinner as Leo had promised — soft sitar music playing, colorful draperies, and Hindu renderings of ancient deities.

"Why did you order so much food?" she asked.

"I wanted you to sample everything I like on the menu. Also, we'll have plenty of leftovers for the weekend. Indian food is similar to Italian, except it's a lot better the next day."

Her face told him she wasn't buying the leftover bit.

"That guy I introduced you to," he said, "as we entered the restaurant, Mark Saltz, he's the owner. He also owns the Green Earth next door. He found himself a little strapped for cash about six months ago when he was opening the Indian restaurant. I loaned him five grand, had my lawyer draw up a promissory note and a contract. I get a hundred bucks a month in credit, usable at the health food store and/or here. I pay full retail and if I don't use the full hundred, it doesn't carry over. I still had $45 credit for this month, so hence the large order tonight."

"Wow, are you a loan shark or just a good pal?"

"The full five thousand is due at the end of the year. If he doesn't pay, I become 51% owner of the Green Earth, which is what I expect will happen."

"At least it explains why I've never seen you pay for anything next door. But what makes you think he won't pay you?"

Leo looked deeply into her eyes. "If I tell you, you have to promise you'll take it to the grave." The comment stopped her cold. Leo waited.

"Okay," she said. "I promise, Mr. Mafia Don."

He smiled, as he'd been doing since he first met her. "Mark likes to dabble in heroin. Thinks if he just uses it on an occasional weekend, he can control it, but I know that is very unlikely. Only one or two in a hundred can manage that feat."

"Oh, I hate needles."

"Mostly, he's what I call a weekend chipper."

"What the hell is that?"

"He injects it with a needle but he doesn't *mainline* it, which means injecting it directly into a vein. Instead, he injects into a muscle. The high is not quite as intense but it lasts longer. Mark believes that by chipping, he's far less likely to get hooked. I stopped by his apartment once during the loan negotiations, and he and his girlfriend were smoking it on aluminum foil. That's called *chasing the dragon*. He offered some to me that day, but I don't like the throwing-up part, so I declined."

"You've never tried it, have you, Leo?"

He hesitated, then said, "I've tried everything at least once."

"I've been with you a full week now, but I know almost nothing about you."

"Nothing to see here, folks, so let's just move along."

She was silent and looked sad.

"What's the matter?" he asked. He was starting to really like this young lady and didn't want to see her gloomy. But still she was quiet. Finally, he asked, "What did Karl tell you about me?" He could almost hear her thinking about how to answer, how much to reveal.

"He told me you were married to a black woman and have a seven-year-old son. And that you know more about drugs than anyone he's ever met. That you always have some of the best smoke on the planet, and that you are one of the smartest, most interesting people he knows. Oh, and that you're a lousy trumpet player."

"Ouch! That really hurts."

"But it's because you don't practice enough, he says, and have an underdeveloped embouchure."

"Did he really use that word?" Leo asked, smiling.

"I don't have a clue what it means, but that's what he said."

Leo laughed. His first thought was that although Angela was, in fact, African-American, she's far from black. In that community, she would be described as "high yella." Their son Clifford had blue eyes and curly blond hair. But Leo said nothing. They'd been so intimate this past week, the last thing he wanted to talk about with her, was his wife.

"Hey, what's today, Friday?" asked Leo, deftly changing the subject. "Because Friday night is when I pull out my 'special stash'."

"I thought you've been pulling that out every night," she said, playfully.

Her bawdy comment surprised him. He put his arm around her and whispered in her ear, "You are such a hussy. And a wanton wench. And those are the two things I love most about you."

"Oh, Leo, you are terrible, but what about your special stash?

He had her attention, and he enjoyed holding forth on his favorite topic. As they ate, he spoke. He told her he loved experimenting with different smokes, blending grass and hash from around the world until he found a unique and exotic taste. The blend they were about to smoke, he said, consisted of two types of marijuana and two different hashes. One grass was 'purple bud' from the Hawaiian island of Maui, grown by his astrology teacher who was rumored to be the bastard son of Charlie Chaplin – more about him later. Resin from weed that was grown on the Cambodian/Thailand border. One hashish was red-Lebanese made exclusively for the royal family of Syria.

"The other," he said, "well, don't ask me how I got it. It's made in a monastery outside of Katmandu, Nepal, thus the name Nepalese Temple Balls."

"Excuse me?" she said, grinning.

"Now Laura, get your mind out of the gutter. We're not talking about body parts."

He explained that these items were made in small batches and almost never leave the country. These 'Temple Balls' came in all sizes from little bigger than a marble to larger than an egg. Not that long ago, he'd bought a very large Temple Ball, almost five ounces. He shaved little bits off with a single-edged razor blade. Before long, he noticed the color and texture began to change from light brown and hard to black and gummy. He knew right away that it was pure opium in the center.

"I still have most of it, but there's no opium in my 'special blend'."

"Okay, Professor of Highness, why not?"

"Because opium has to be smoked separately in an opium pipe."

She was taking it all in like an enraptured student at a college lecture.

"I'm very fond of Nepalese hash," Leo said. "It was the first cannabis I ever smoked. I was twelve at the time, but it wasn't a Temple Ball. It was something called Nepalese 'fingers'."

By this time, the slim Indian waitress in a sari, had packaged their leftovers, and the couple left without paying, according to the agreement Leo had with the owner.

Back at his apartment, she put the food in the fridge as he walked over to his built-in bookshelves to the right of the fireplace, and took out a 33' record album.

"Ever hear of Thelonious Monk?" he asked, when she plopped down on the sofa.

"How can you forget a name like that?"

"Well, now you're going to hear the music of a true genius."

The album was "The Thelonious Monk Orchestra Live at Town Hall." He started the record at a low volume while he filled the pipe with his special blend.

"Well, so far I've learned a lot about dope," she said, "but very little about Leo. Care to enlighten me further. You certainly are a fascinating man to someone who's been very few places and not done very much."

"Sure, after we take a hit, I'll give you a brief synopsis of my life and times. If I can still speak…."

———◆———

Born in a mud hut in the Pamir Mountains of Tajikistan, Liev Maastricht (Sol) was destined to live a life of adventure! It started on July 25, 1944, when Zigmund and Dora welcomed their firstborn. They escaped the Warsaw Ghetto on October 1, 1939, days after Poland's surrender. Captured by a Russian patrol in the Ukraine, they were sent to a Siberian gulag. Fate brought them to the streets of Baltimore in 1951.

In 1968, Sol's dear friend Roland Kirk (pre-Rahsaan) invited Sol to the live recording of Roland and Jimi Hendrix to take place in Ronnie Scott's club at Soho, London. When Roland introduced Sol said to Jimi, "Sol, here, is the hippest white boy in America!" Jimi replied, "High praise, indeed, from the maestro, himself."

and
STREETS OF BALTIMORE

Two Stories by

Sol Gumpricht

DWG

CAROL SIYAHI HICKS

Gifts from the Garden
(Two excerpts)

The Weight and Levity of Snow:
Living in the Moment while Waiting for Spring

Goldenrod languished beneath the weight of snow. It bent toward an earth hard with winter and waiting. The earth held its breath for spring. But the land was glowing in its ghostly garb, draped over the dried brown stalks of my flower garden and the fields beyond, stalks transfixed, frozen in form by the frosts of late fall and early winter.

My cross-country skis bit the crust of the snow on the path my husband, George, cut with his John Deere tractor, past the garden and through the once-lush greenness of the grasses and prairie plants in the back acres of our property. I watched the frozen forms of the plants, once alive with purples and yellows, whites and golds, browns and greens. Now there was only brown and white. Form and purity. Earth and water. Substance and air. Life and death. This moment.

I always have loved snow days in Southwest Ohio, especially because we have so precious few of them. When the snow would come in plenitude—more than a dusting, enough on which to ski—I would feel unbridled joy. I found I would do almost anything to grab hold of the moment and rush outside with my twenty-year-old pair of skis to kick and glide my way across our five acres of land. I would go in the dark if I had to, get up early to ski before work, or take off from my job to spend time playing in the snow. Because later that day or tomorrow, it all could be gone. Snow in Ohio, if you love it, forces you to live in the moment. It is a gift of fullness sprung from meagerness.

So round and round I skied. First along the fence line with our neighbor who has the horses. Then along the boundary with the neighbor at a distance who has the disturbingly blue house in an otherwise earth-toned landscape. Then along the fence between us and the neighbor with the goats—three or four varieties of curious, bearded, and horned fellows with their watchful eyes and rounded bellies. Finally up a little hill and along the west edge of the pond George dug a few years back with his tractor. And then round again.

It was not unusual for me to round the field for an hour at a time. I usually ended up by taking several runs down the larger hill beside our house, down toward the pond, narrowly missing its icy surface with its half-frozen fish waiting like the earth for spring. I could glide almost to the barn at the north side of our property, having started from the southernmost end. I marked my ski tracks to try for progressively farther finishes. It was a contest I had with myself, finding ways to increase speed, momentum, and ultimately distance, marking the end point of my final glide.

And when I had spent all my time and energy, I climbed in herringbone form back up the hill to deposit myself sweaty and exhausted, but strangely invigorated, in my home that opened to the land all white and full of form and sky and light.

The Intrinsic Readiness of Spring

Spring was long this year. In Southwestern Ohio spring frequently has lasted only two or three weeks. This time, however, the cool to moderate temperatures and the rain held on well into June. The spring flowers bloomed exuberantly, and my cool-temperature-loving pansies had an unusually extended season.

The coolness kept the mosquitoes at bay and delayed the planting of tomato and pepper plants. The weeds, however, grew in abundance, as did the grass. At times it seemed as if all George and I did was pull weeds and mow grass. But it was wonderful to have this long period of gentle temperatures and lush spring growth.

Later, because of the protracted spring, summer flowers started blooming while the spring ones hung on. Daylilies mingled with pansies, hollyhock with flowering sage, flowering yucca with chrysanthemum—a chaotic mix of seasons colliding in my Ohio garden.

There is something about the start of spring that stirs the soul. It is as if your innermost self emerges from hibernation to stand in the presence of life opening impatiently around you. The spring bulbs can hardly wait to leave the underground as they tear up through soil and explode into the warming air. The grass starts to become that color we call "spring green," like no other green I've seen outside of the British Isles except at this time of year.

The trees and bushes with their tight buds ache now to expand into their new foliage—and frequently do so too soon. But for the plants that wait, oh what a joy they are in their young foliage all yellow-green and fresh.

There is an intrinsic readiness about spring that comes from long waiting, a readiness that we humans experience as well. This feeling, it seems to me, is part of our deep human need for change. We are at our best—or worst, if this is our inclination—when we are responding to the unexpected. It calls up something firmly instinctual to which our whole system—physical, emotional, and spiritual—responds. The shift of seasons forces change upon us humans who tend to resist the very thing that enlivens and expands us.

And then there is the simple enjoyment of spring's special mixture of sensual pleasures. The scent of lilacs behind the house. The brush of a gentle breeze against the skin. The intensity of color in the rows of tulips and in the lawn with its haunting green spilling down the hill toward the pond, dazzling under a sunlit and lavishly blue sky.

Carol Siyahi Hicks is an avid gardener, a longtime backpacker, and the author of *Gifts from the Garden*, which probes the subtleties of everyday experiences to explore our relationship to nature and the mysteries of life. She recently completed a novel, *The Color of Acceptance*, centered on the Civil Rights era of the 1960s and 1970s. The story illumines a gifted young woman's quest for her identity and for acceptance. Carol's career includes years as a newspaper and magazine journalist, as a university communications officer (where she worked with national and international news media), and as communications vice president of a large community foundation. In earlier years, she served as managing editor of *The Antioch Review* and co-editor of *Fiction International.* She has won many national and regional awards for her writing and communications work, most recently from *Writer's Digest*'s Annual Writing Competition for her poetry and personal essays.

Available on Amazon. Copyright 2021. All rights reserved.

DWG

DAVE EASBY

Lack of Precision Air

Anne and I were talking to the concierge at the Sultan Sands Resort. "Around here," she said, "we all call it 'Lack of Precision Air.'" She chuckled as she tapped the keyboard, confirming our flight from Zanzibar to Dar el Salaam.

It had been a TripAdvisor post—*Precision Air is the most reliable of the smaller African airlines*—that had convinced us to choose this company from the limited options available. But we now suspected the recommendation had been posted by Precision Air's CEO.

I suppose that in hindsight '*most* reliable' should have sent up some red flags. Exactly how high was the bar set by the '*less* reliable' competitors? And what exactly did 'most reliable' mean? After all, the recommendations for carriers like Delta, United, and Air Canada highlight the quality of the food or the service. They don't flaunt virtues like 'the flights generally depart and arrive as scheduled, and land at their intended destinations.'

The first clue about what was in store for us was a terse email from our travel agent that had arrived a week earlier. We were sitting in a tent in the middle of the Masai

Mara Game Reserve: "There has been a change in your flight from Nairobi to Zanzibar. It has been moved from May 7 to May 8." The *pro forma* note did provide reassurance that we would receive new E-tickets "within two weeks of your new departure date."

"How do you plan to accomplish this," was my snarky reply, "when our new flight is only three days away?"

"This address is not set up to receive incoming mail," was the automated reply.

There was a seven-hour time difference between Kenya and our travel agent back home in Canada. The resort had internet only four hours a day, and it worked only if there was a cloudless sky and if none of the other fifty resort guests were attempting to retrieve their emails at the same time.

Would we have to stew in this heat for two more weeks?

"They cancel flights all the time during the low season," Tom, our Tour Director, calmly advised us over lunch. "It depends if they get enough customers to fill the plane."

Anne and I had chosen to take a group tour to Kenya rather than venture there on our own. It was a decision we were thankful for every time we passed through metal detectors on our way into each hotel or restaurant. But we would be traveling on to Zanzibar by ourselves—or at least we hoped we would be traveling—assuming that *Precision Air* had found enough folks to fill the May 8 flight.

"Let me make a few calls," Tom added. "I'll see what I can find out."

It was two more sleepless nights before Tom greeted us with a solution. The Nairobi offices of Precision Air, KLM, and Delta, the airlines that might allow us to cut our losses and just head back to Canada with the group, were all closed for the weekend.

"I talked to the folks at Precision Air," Tom announced proudly, "and we came up with a solution."

I wasn't sure what 'folks' Tom was referring to. Perhaps the company president had torn himself away from posting glowing reviews on the internet to answer the phone. Or perhaps the pilot had taken the call after he had finished refueling the plane.

"We will drop you off at the airport," Tom continued, "on the day of your original flight. You need to go to the check-in counter and pretend that you don't know about the flight change. They will give you a boarding pass for the flight next morning and put you up in a hotel for the night."

"Pretend?"

"Yeah, trust me. It'll work just fine."

At least we had a plan, even if it meant that our four-day sojourn to Zanzibar was now cut to three, if we made it at all.

Mid-afternoon Abdi, our driver, dropped us off at Jomo Kenyatta International Airport, well, at least at the airport parking garage. The garage was serving as a temporary terminal since the original building had burnt down several months earlier. We pushed our way through the mass of humanity that crowded around the baggage x-ray machine: young Muslim men in white chambrays and grey kufis, African women with brightly coloured headwraps and long flowing robes, and businessmen in tailored suits. All this, just on the way into the terminal. Abdi agreed to wait a few minutes in case there was a hitch in Tom's plan—our being untrained as actors—not that we would have known where to find Abdi in the chaos if there was a *hitch*.

Given the high level of security; this was our second time being searched, the first having taken place on the highway into the airport. We had been advised to arrive five hours before departure and were already two hours late. We prayed that wouldn't derail the little white lie that Tom had negotiated with his mysterious contact at Precision Air.

There was, of course, no check-in counter for Precision Air. There were counters for Emirates Air, Ethiopian Air, and Kenya Airways which, if my memory served me right, were the 'less reliable' options disparaged in TripAdvisor. The first two agents we urgently asked just shrugged blankly.

"Precision Airlines? I don't know of them…."

We shoved our way to Kenya Airways.

"Let me check," said the rep with a nametag that identified her as Julie. "Can you please have a seat over there?" She pointed to a packed waiting area.

We plodded through. I must have checked my watch a dozen times eyeing Julie scurry around surely in search of anyone who might know someone who knew someone who had a friend who worked at *Precision Air*. The few minutes grace that our driver Abdi had promised had long since evaporated, content that he had done his duty in leaving us on our own with tickets for a flight that didn't exist, and with nowhere to stay for the night. He must have assumed we were seasoned thespians.

"Come with me please," Julie said at last, seeming to have achieved success in her search. "Yes, I located your airline, but sorry to say, your flight has been cancelled. I did, however, manage to book you on a flight in the morning."

We feigned surprise just as Tom had directed but were probably less than convincing. We guessed this was probably not Julie's first rodeo, so she knew the drill.

"Hotel?" I asked as the boarding passes spewed out of the printer.

"Yes, of course, but we must go to another area for that. Can you follow me please?"

Now, on our way through the mob, we noticed a Precision Air office with a tiny, blurred sign. Hauling our luggage, we followed Julie in that direction, but she astounded us by moving right past it out of the building. It made no sense—were we on our way to an abduction? We struggled to keep up as she sashayed through a parking lot, greeting and hugging friends along the way.

We crossed the busy highway and hesitantly went through the back door of the drab concrete block garage structure, which we were greatly relieved served as a terminal. Julie argued to no avail with the security staff that we didn't need our luggage scanned since we were actually leaving the airport.

"Here is your voucher for a hotel and meals," the rep said, finally handing me an endless ream of paperwork. I silently thanked Tom and his Secret Santa at Precision Air. The voucher was from Kenya Air, but who was I to question why they were ponying up for one of their competitors. Julie stood there patiently before escorting us back through security and across the highway to the waiting bus—*Waiting* being the operative word, since the driver insisted on staying until the half hour even though we were the only passengers. We could not in good conscience allow Julie to leave us without a serious tip, so I rummaged through my wallet and slipped her a twenty-dollar bill.

The Panari Hotel is the closest there is to an airport hotel in Nairobi. It would have been a state-of-the-art hotel – back in 1963. Since we seemed to be the only guests other than a few travel refugees cashing in vouchers from other cancelled Precision Air flights, the staff was uncomfortably attentive. They followed us around, tending to our every need – even needs we didn't know we had. It was a thirty-minute drive from the airport, but would be a significantly longer one going back next morning, given the need for every vehicle on the highway into the airport to deposit all its passengers for inspection. That, and the need to report to the airport four hours before flight time (the lack of traffic early in the morning buying us an hour's grace) meant a 4:00 AM wake-up call.

And so, several hours later we climbed the steps and boarded Precision Air Flight 710. On the tarmac, the gentle roar of the engines starting up lulled us to sleep. Zanzibar beckoned in our dreams, and suddenly just as images of white sand and turquoise waters played in my head, the engine roar stopped. Surely, I hadn't slept through the whole flight.

"There is a problem with the control tower," the pilot announced.

My fingers dug into the armrests as I imagined what kind of 'problem' there might be. After all, there had been two bombs go off in Nairobi during our visit, and we had come as close to being strip searched as I'd ever want to be upon entering every hotel and restaurant.

"What's going on?" I asked the steward as he emerged from the cockpit, resplendent in his crisp lime green and bright yellow uniform.

"We forgot to file a flight plan," he mumbled, staring at the floor. "So, the control tower won't let us take off. But it shouldn't be long."

The gentleman in the seat across from us nodded as if this would have been his guess.

"As usual," he said, opening a newspaper.

Apparently, he was a member of the Precision Air Frequent Flyers Program.

As we waited, and waited, I imagined our friend Julie from yesterday strutting across the parking lot in her high heels, heading to the control tower with the flight plan – likely scribbled on the back of a cocktail napkin.

So, given our experience getting to Zanzibar, we were relieved three days later when the Sultan Sands concierge advised us that, "Yes, you are confirmed on the Precision Air Flight back to Dar el Salaam. And it is scheduled to depart on time. By the way, how long is your stop-over in Dar?"

"Five hours," I replied, still grateful that the long layover provided some flexibility just on the off chance there might be further problems. After all, Dar el Salaam was our last stop in Africa before we headed home on KLM – which I understood to be one of the most 'reliable' of the international airlines.

"That's good," she added. "At least, there is a Kenya Air flight that leaves an hour after yours. Just in case."

But Precision Air Flight 471 was on schedule, or at least when we arrived at the Zanzibar Airport later that afternoon. The giant 'Z' on the bright green control tower greeted us. And to both our relief and amazement there was actually a check-in counter that said *Precision Air.*

"Have a good flight," the attendant said as he handed us our boarding passes and we said goodbye to our luggage. Hopefully not for the last time. This was hardly O'Hare or La Guardia; the only businesses were a shop selling tacky souvenirs and a snack bar selling samosas for the folks trying to dispose of the last of their Tanzanian Shillings, useful for little more than bookmarks the moment one set foot outside the country.

There was also a washroom, but with an attendant who demanded a tip before letting you enter. Woe be the traveler who had wolfed down a full breakfast or had that second cup of coffee to divest themselves of the last of their funds at the souvenir shop. All of this was beyond the security gate, so we did the usual discarding of wallets and watches and shoes and belts, and made our way through to the Boarding Gate, the word *Gate* being singular.

"Precision Air Flight 471 to Dar el Salaam is now ready for boarding," the PA system blared, to our amazement precisely on schedule. But it would have been just as easy for the agent to individually inform the dozen or so people who now sauntered up to the gate.

"We're 1A and 1B," I said to Anne as I examined the boarding passes on our way to the front of the line.

I held out the boarding card to the gate agent, but she dismissed me with a wave of her hand and moved on to the next person in line.

I tried showing her my boarding pass and passport. Boarding pass and tourist visa. Each attempt got a wordless rebuke. The bright yellow and green plane with the leaping gazelle painted on its tail stood shimmering in the hot sun. Tantalizingly out of reach – so near and yet so far.

"What is she looking for?' I pleaded to the man behind me in line.

"Your departure tax sticker," he replied as he handed her his boarding card with the bright red sticker. "You have to go back through security to get it."

The sounds of "Last Call for Precision Air Flight 471" rang in my ears as I bulldozed my way back through the metal detector, scattering staff and passengers in equal numbers. Lights flashed. Alarms sounded. I half expected to be tackled by the Tanzanian army.

"Go ahead, I'll just let you back through," I heard the security guard say to someone behind me and assumed they were talking to Anne who calmly followed along.

Payment, as is the case in many countries, was only payable in US funds, fortunate since I had spent the last of my local currency on half a dozen samosas and a trip to the john. I searched frantically through the umpteen pockets in my cargo pants. Making sure to equally distribute our valuables had seemed like a good idea when we'd boarded a cab at the resort that morning, but was now proving to be less than a stroke of genius. The minute hand on my watch raced forward. The attendant tapped her pen impatiently. I finally retrieved a twenty from pocket number eight and plunked it down on the counter.

True to his word, the security waved us through belt and shoes and all, and we rushed through the now empty boarding area with our boarding passes now adorned with the precious red stickers.

There were only two empty seats when we boarded the plane – the engines roared and the fight plan had obviously been filed. But neither of the vacant places were 1A or 1B.

"Just sit anywhere," the stewardess barked. "It's only a twenty-minute flight."

I filled the twenty minutes regaling my seatmate with my sad tale of cancelled flights, missing flight plans, and departure taxes.

"I'm not sure why Precision Air don't just add the tax to the ticket price like everyone else" he said when I stopped for breath. "Africa. You know you were lucky there were any seats left. The flight started in Arusha and the stewardess told me that they weren't expecting that many people to board in Zanzibar. You do know," he added in a conspiratorial whisper, "us locals all call it *Lack* of Precision Air."

Dave Easby spends his summers in New Brunswick, Canada and his winters in Dunedin, Florida with his wife Anne. He retired in 2005 after a thirty-year career with the Canadian and New Brunswick Governments. Since much of that time was spent working on speeches and briefing notes for Ministers and other Senior Officials, he decided to try writing non-fiction for a change in his retirement years. He has two books out: *They Tore Down the Russell Hotel – A Story of Change in Small Town Mexico* and *Mystery Monkeys and Unstable Discs – A Snowbird's Sketches of the Sunshine State*. The above story is from his forthcoming effort: *Travels with My Angst.*

DWG

JOHN WHALEN

Summer Camp with the Big Boys

In the summer of 1968, war may have been raging in the jungles of Asia, the boulevards of Paris, and the cities of America, but life in the wilds of southern Georgia proceeded at its usual quiet, lazy pace. Fort Benning prided itself as the premiere infantry post in the Army. Trainees learned the latest in jungle fighting, survival tactics, weaponry, parachuting, and whatever else grunts needed to know.

I received only short glimpses at that *whatever* because I was among the support troops. Soldiers from my company ran the commissaries, fixed the refrigerators, monitored the drinking water, and groomed the golf courses. You name it, we did it, anything that was not a normal military function.

I worked eight-hours a day, five days a week, with a civilian electrician. I could go a week without seeing my platoon sergeant even once. So long that no one complained about our work, my platoonmates and I were as free-floating as those hippies on the outside. We did make minor concessions to Uncle Sam.

I wore combat boots and olive-drab fatigues while on duty, made up my bunk army-style each morning, and might pull guard duty one night a month on a weekend. When we returned to our barracks after work, we all changed into our civvies, civilian clothes. That time of year, civvies meant Bermuda shorts and tee-shirts. We would exercise a modicum of discretion however — no peace symbols or Che Guevara faces on the tees.

why Our only other apparent military restraint was that none of us could leave the post without a pass signed by our First Sergeant. Passes for an evening came easily. He signed a stack of them ahead of time, so the office clerk could hand them out to whoever asked. Several of the guys spent most evenings in downtown Columbus, Georgia. So long as they were back through the guard gate by six in the morning, all was copacetic.

Everyone knew the best spots in Columbus. The Army in its inscrutable wisdom posted outside our Captain's office a list of off-limits addresses. That's right, street name and number of each of the establishments in Columbus, and in Phenix City, Alabama too, that soldiers were forbidden to patronize. Need I mention the most popular addresses with GIs in both cities?

I am relating all this as preliminary to my story, so that you can appreciate that everything you always thought about army regimentation and discipline did not apply in my company. If you refuse to accept that, you will find the rest of what I am telling you overblown or not at all credible. But I swear, every word is true. Well, mostly.

One civilian amenity lacking even for us was privacy. Our barracks was one large room with thirty cots, thirty footlockers, and multiple fans to mitigate a Georgia summer without air conditioning. My bunkmate was Phil, a PFC, Private First Class, from rural Kentucky. During the day, he ran the projection booth at the twenty-four-hour movie theater. "We may doze, but we never close."

Evenings, he spent complaining to me about his family back in the hills. His father drank non-stop. His mother ran around with every moonshiner in town. With coalmines closing up, bootlegging was the most profitable enterprise around, most profitable enterprise for males anyway. With Phil gone, his little brother now alone bore the brunt of his parents' never-ending battles.

One weekend, Phil received a four-day pass to go home to see what he could do about the ever-escalating violence in his household. The following Wednesday morning, reveille awoke me to find a fifteen-year-old Phil look-alike in the bunk above me. Oh, I forgot to mention, reveille and lights-out were two more of our few concessions to army protocol. Real Phil was just crawling out from a previously-empty bunk across the center aisle.

"What's going on here?" I asked, actually whispered, giving Phil the courtesy of not broadcasting news of our new boarder until I had a handle on the facts. My question was unnecessary; the facts were self-evident.

"Mike," Phil said to me, "ma li'l brother here's gonna bunk up a couple days with us till we can figure where he can go to be safe." He introduced me and five other gathered, yawning GIs to the outsider. "He can get vittles at the cantina. Lots of guys wear civvies there. Then he'll huddle up the day with me in the projection room at the movin' picture house. By sundown, we'll have done concocted some plan." He paused and sighed. "Hopefully."

I just shook my head in disbelief and went about my morning rituals. That day will live in my memory forever, not just because of Phil and his brother. Bobby Kennedy, brother to the fallen president, died of gunshot wounds after decisively winning the California primary the previous day, a win which would have assured him the Democratic presidential nomination and likely the presidency.

At supper in the mess hall, I saw ahead of me in line Fake Phil in Real Phil's uniform with PFC stripe and all. Both had that Bob-Hope ski-jump nose and pencil-thin lips. Each sported jet-black crew cuts. But where Phil was thin, his brother was scrawny — and two inches shorter. Fake Phil found an empty table at the far corner of the hall and sat facing the wall. I joined him.

"So how did your first day in the army go?" I asked.

"I thought watching movin' pictures all the day long, I'd be happier than a skeeter at the skinny-dipping crick. But third time through *Planet of the Apes* just about deep-fried ma brain. I was fixing to start cheering for the monkeys."

Real Phil arrived, having gone through the other chow line. Within a couple minutes, the table filled with curious GIs from our barracks. Phil quieted the gawkers, swore them to secrecy, then explained, starting with an honest description of his brother's plight back home.

"Our older brother, he did flee to Detroit to work in the motorcar factories when he was seventeen. I volunteered for the draft the day after I graduated high school. We both wanted to get the hell outta Kentuck so fast that we din't give no thought what would happen to the li'l brother we left back in the holler. Well, sweet Jesus, it happened. So here he is."

"Phil, how are you going to pull this off?" one fellow asked. "I mean, your brother looks fifteen. What if people see the two of you together? What if someone asks to see his military ID?"

"I done informed the clerk in the First-Sergeant's office that I lost ma ID in the laundry. He writ me up a temporary card. Bro here can use that for a day or two. If he's gonna be here a piece, he can impersonate me at the front gate and get a new valid ID, or kinda valid anyways."

"Phil, you have to be violating a dozen army regulations," one of the other platoon mates piped in. "You both could be in deep trouble."

"In trouble for impersonating a Private First Class, how damn serious can that be? If the army kicks me out, then we'll both go to Detroit. Whatever happens, it's a damn sight better than where we come from."

I could only smile at all this. So many men our age were flooding universities, faking chronic illnesses, and fleeing to Canada to avoid the draft, but here at Fort Benning, a boy was trying to sneak into the military.

By lights out that evening, everyone in the barracks had met Fake Phil, marveled at the boldness of Real Phil's plan, and, more importantly, agreed to accept the newcomer and keep his mouth shut.

Thursday, Week Two of the conspiracy — at least, I remember it as Thursday — it was the day that the Feds convicted Dr. Spock of conspiring to aid draft resistors. The man who wrote the users' manual on how to raise America's kids was heading to jail for warping their malleable young minds. Well anyway, I ate lunch alone with Fake Phil that noon.

"So how are things really going?" I asked. "Any close calls?"

"None yet. The Spec-5 who bosses the movin' picture house is in on our devices. It don't trouble him none. I can lounge around with the other watchers and enjoy ma self. But even with doubled features, sitting through four or five of them pictures a day begins to drag a fella down. I mean, how many times running can a body watch *Rosemary's Baby*? Don't be shooked up if I howl out tonight in my damn sleep."

"Well, you won't be alone. Several in the barracks are finishing out their enlistments here after returning from a year in Asia. You already know a shriek at three in the morning is not unheard of around here."

"I got so fulled up of movin' pictures," he continued, "that I went to the crafts center yesterday in the p.m. and made ceramic critters for three hours. Today, the fella who runs the place, he's gonna show me how to work the lathe and make fancy walking sticks. He told me to come any time I want since he's in the platoon, your platoon."

"The platoon, your platoon, huh? If this charade is going to work, it's *our* platoon, yours and mine. You're just another of the guys."

"You telling me that I can run out some p.m. to one of those hopping honkytonks in town with the other guys?"

"Well, that's not my decision to make." I started into the first sentence about maintaining the values our parents gave us, but stopped when I realized that none of what I was about to say applied to his parents. That evening, Real Phil, Fake Phil, and I played cutthroat euchre till lights-out.

Friday evening, Real Phil pulled guard duty. With him out of sight to monitor activities, several fellows kidnapped his brother and took him to town with them. About two in the morning, Fake Phil woke me as he tried, without much success, climbing into the upper bunk.

Even in the dark, I could see his Cheshire Cat smile stretching from earlobe to earlobe. At reveille three hours later, he still resembled the cat that had just swallowed the canary. By noon, the entire barracks knew every detail of that night on the town. I will pass over further description in deference to propriety.

On Week Three, Fake Phil started going to work with me. The civilian electrician I apprenticed with could not care less. He had witnessed enough bizarre behavior from the military that he chalked this up as just one more example. By the time the man picked the two of us up in the morning he had already reported to his shop and received his day's assignments. Fake Phil was a fast learner; by the end of the first day he really was helping. By Friday afternoon, he was changing out switches and light fixtures on his own. In fact, we had to slow down, or the chief electrician would start criticizing my civilian partner for accomplishing too many tasks a day and making all the other electricians look bad. Worse yet, he might discover we were harboring a stowaway.

Working together gave us plenty of time to talk. Regardless of his faulty grammar, Fake Phil was a smart guy. He had dreams. His main one, which he was in the process of fulfilling, was getting far away from his parents. He wanted to live with his older brother in Detroit, finish high school there, and maybe even start college.

"Since Phil left home," he told me, "this year has been the ugliest damn time of ma life. Mammy and Pappy have forever been baiting each other, nit-picking, complaining, just being hell all the time. This spring, their talking and swearing battles, they done turned into mad-dog fights with throwing punches and bottles and what-have-ya. As the only youngin left at home, I got it both barrels from each of 'em. Mammy would apologize to me later — assuring me it weren't no fault of mine but the fault of Pappy. Then he'd do the same, reverse like, after he sobered up. I'd try my damnedest to console, comfort, or whatever I thought might still the flood. Let me tell ya, trying to be the only adult in the house, it's like riding an ornery colt bareback and stark naked yourself. I kinda like it here on an army base full up with soldiers. It's a heap more peaceful."

Later, Fake Phil would rotate through several jobs with other platoon members. His favorite days were with the Graves Registration crew who oversaw the cemetery; I hoped not because they drank and watched soap operas all afternoon.

His fourth week here, I remember every detail: the peaceful Poor Peoples' March on Washington, followed by police with tear gas and bulldozers busting up Resurrection City where thousands of other Blacks and activists had camped out for six weeks on the National Mall, on the most sacred strip of grass in America. That same week, Jim Hines broke the ten-second barrier by running the hundred meters in nine-point-nine seconds. But why I remember that week so clearly is because that was when disaster struck, for me at least. I, but not Real Phil, received notice to start seven days of VN training.

Back then, all GIs, and likely most civilians too, knew precisely what the initials VN stood for. But GIs knew also what followed shortly after a week of said training. The thought of maneuvering obstacle courses, shooting M-16 rifles, eating cold C-rations, and sleeping on bare ground for seven nights repelled me but captivated Fake Phil. He begged his brother to figure a way he could go along with me — along for the training that is, not for what certainly would soon follow.

A PFC who took the training two weeks earlier told Real Phil that the sergeants in charge do call attendance. If everyone on their list is present, that's all they care about. Never would it occur to them that a person not on the list would sneak in for training.

Before sunrise Monday morning of Week Five, Fake Phil and I, along with three others from the platoon, boarded the open back of a two-and-a-half-ton truck for the fifteen-mile ride to the training fields even further into the middle of nowhere. Real Phil had received promotion to Spec-4 a few days earlier, so Fake Phil's uniform signaled that he now outranked most of us on the truck.

When we lined up in formation at training headquarters, Sergeant Gonzales, our sergeant for the week, a muscular man with pockmarked face, looked us over, then delivered the same speech I remember from basic training.

Here and in episodes to follow, I somewhat sanitize the man's language. Maybe more than somewhat.

"For the next seven days, I am your father and your mother, your brother and your sister. But sure as hell, I ain't going to be your girlfriend, so don't try screwing me." Then he turned and complained to the nearby lieutenant, loud enough so I heard, "Fresh fish get fresher every year." Beyond that, he paid no particular attention to Fake Phil's obvious youth. Most of us there could have passed for high school juniors ourselves.

First day was all classroom orientation. Little did we know that was going to be the last time we saw the inside of a building for a week. That night we bedded down with nothing between us and bumpy ground but our ponchos. In the morning, Fake Phil said he snoozed like a wildcat with its belly full of gopher meat, which I took to mean that he slept well. He told me that, many nights, he would sleep on the grass in his backyard to avoid his father's drunken rages.

Second day started with learning how to disassemble, clean, and reassemble our M-16 rifles, practicing till we could do it blindfolded. Then the dreaded obstacle course. We shimmied up twenty-foot ropes, climbed sheer cliffs, and waded through swamps supposedly infested with alligators and water moccasins. That evening the sergeant informed us we were eating rats; Fake Phil said it tasted like possum to him.

I suspected it was just yesterday's overcooked chicken, overcooked a second time. Except for a queasy stomach after such a vigorous day and disgusting meal, even I slept soundly until about three when, appropriate for our training, a Georgia cloudburst mimicked an Asian monsoon. At reveille an hour before daybreak, we all howled at the driving rain just like Jumpin' Jack Flash. Sergeant Gonzales put a quick stop to that.

"Your M-16s, I bet they're full of water and mud. What if you came under attack right now? What do you plan to do when your rifles jam? Hit the enemies over the head with your gas masks? Don't you sorry bastards know what your ponchos are for? Drop right here where you stand for two-hundred sit-ups while I think how I get through your thick skulls that the purpose of ponchos is to keep dry your most important items, which are not your bodies." We all looked down at soaked ground at our feet.

Fake Phil turned to me and said, "I kept ma rifle wrapped in ma poncho all night. It's as dry as Pappy after a three-day stay in the slammer. Do I have to do the sit-ups too?"

"Never argue with a sergeant," I whispered. "Do the exercises and shut up." We all dropped to our knees, Sergeant Gonzales too, and floundered in the mush as he counted out the repetitions at his pace. By the time he and Fake Phil reached their two-hundred together, I was still at one-fifty. But we all stood up anyway, mud covered toe to head to hair to face to mouth.

"Okay, you sad sacks, we're going for a two-mile run to build up your appetites for breakfast. Suit up with backpacks." Jogging in five-pounds of muddy combat boots is bad enough, but the seventy-pound packs are equivalent to a fourth-grader piggy-backing the whole way.

227

By the time most of us finished the run, Fake Phil had already gone through the chow line and was searching for a dry spot to sit.

We spent the rest of the day on the rifle range. At lunch of cold C-rations, I sat on the soggy ground with Fake Phil and told him, "You're too good. You'll get noticed. Start missing the bull's eye some."

"But Mike, I've been hunting my whole damn life. Ma brothers say I can blast a turkey gobbler's head off at a hundred paces. This is the most damn fun I've had since I arrived in these parts, most fun in years. I'm in hillbilly heaven here. And a good day for it too." He puffed up and grinned. "Today's ma birthday. Sixteen whole years on God's good Earth."

"Shhh." I put my index finger up to my mouth. "We don't want anyone to hear that. You're Phil. You're nineteen."

That evening, I drew pound cake in my C-ration box. I shared half of it with Fake Phil. No lighted candle on top, but it was the best I could do. I felt sorry for him, having to celebrate his sixteenth year of life with a bunch of strangers in the middle of the boonies. But he did not seem to mind in the least. Although I did not know it until we returned to civilization, his birthday was the same day the Feds indicted Daniel Ellsberg for leaking the Pentagon Papers.

Day six — as I waited my turn climbing the cliff for at least the tenth time, the sergeant walked over to me. He pointed to Fake Phil half way up. "He's one of the best trainees I've seen all summer. Wish you all had his enthusiasm. I was thinking of recommending him for Ranger

School. But when I checked my list, his name wasn't on it." I tensed up. Drats, we've been discovered. But the sergeant continued. "I called your battalion headquarters yesterday to get the paperwork straight. Their clerk told me they added your buddy to the roster at the last minute." I relaxed. Having a platoon member working in headquarters saved our scheme. "You hover over that boy like a hen guarding her brood."

"Well, Sarge, he and I are bunkmates. The army teaches us to watch our buddies' backs."

"The record says he's nineteen. You're eighteen. He outranks you. When you all washed up in the creek yesterday, I had to notice — he's barely sprouted pin feathers. Whatever the cover story is, I don't buy it. But my job is to train whoever shows up, not to get too nosy." He paused. "So, should I suggest him for Ranger training or not?"

"Sarge, I wish you wouldn't. Can we leave it at that?"

My turn at the cliff was up, so I ran off without awaiting a response. Fake Phil was at the top, helping stragglers like me grope up the last few feet.

Final day — we lined up waiting for the busses to take us back to so-called civilization on main base; Gonzales started handing out certificates for meritorious performances. He called Fake Phil to step forward for winning on the rifle range.

"I don't know what's going on, but good luck, son." He winked at Fake Phil, then looked over at me and winked again. I expelled a deep breath.

July arrived with Fake Phil still with us. Hank Aaron hit his five-hundredth homerun. Five days of riots broke out in Cleveland, with a shoot-out leaving three cops, three Black Nationalists, and one bystander dead. Palestinians highjacked Israeli airliners, twice. John Wayne's *The Green Berets* played endlessly at the movie theater. I hoped its popularity came not from some perceived excellence but from its having been filmed at Fort Benning with real soldiers playing the extras. I also hoped that Fake Phil had not watched it fifteen times. By the end of the month, half of Fort Benning must have heard about the two brothers, but apparently found the story too absurd to credit. Or maybe no one in authority cared. July departed, but Fake Phil stayed.

The August day the Republicans nominated Nixon at their raucous convention in Miami, I received orders to report to the Oakland Army Depot for reassignment to Asia. Two weeks later, the Russians invaded Czechoslovakia. Then, with the Rascals' *People Got to Be Free* at the top of the charts, rioters disrupted the Democratic Convention and trashed half of downtown Chicago along with Humphrey's chances at election. That same night I was aboard a jet flying over the Pacific.

That September day when Detroit's Denny McLain pitched his thirty-first win of the season — a feat last accomplished in 1931 — I put that rifle-range training to use for the first time. I recollect *Hey Jude* being the number-one hit that week. The October night the American sprinters raised their fists in the Black Power Salute during playing of *The Star-Spangled Banner* at the Mexico City Olympics, I received a letter postmarked from an unfamiliar address at Fort Benning.

Dear Mike,

Not much time to write here. Phil left for Berlin in September. I found an army recruiter in Columbus willing to bend the rules and write my age as seventeen. I really am a genuine, certified GI now. Basic training. I seem to accept being away from home and adjusting to new surroundings faster than other recruits. I wonder why.

———◆———

With much appreciated encouragement from other members of the Dunedin Writers Group, John J. Whalen has written a novel about a young man's journey from the boonies of Vietnam to the campus of The Ohio State University just as antiwar protests and riots erupted nationwide in the spring of 1970. John hopes to publish this novel soon. In addition to jogging, biking, and hiking, he enjoys writing short stories, especially about the effects of historic events on everyday people. He is a retired mechanical engineer, living in Safety Harbor, Florida, but spending summers in the Finger Lakes region of upstate New York.

DWG

MARY ANNE BARRY

The O'Keafe Family

Chapter One
"Top of the morning to you!"

June 1975 - Philadelphia

Oh, I wish Finn would stay in his own bed. He crawls into mine every morning, kisses my cheek, and pulls at my eyelids to see if I am conscious. Finn is a chubby little guy with a mop of curly black hair. I snuggle up to him and wrap my arms around his body, squeezing him until he giggles.

Finn shares a room with Patrick and Conor but, they don't let him into their beds, so he walks down the hallway into my room. He is the baby of the family. I can hardly believe he will be five at the end of September.

"Finn," she said. "Just let me rest my eyes for a few more minutes," she told him, hoping he'd get bored and leave me alone.

"Teenie, wake up. I have to go pee-pee."

Teenie rubbed the sleep out of her eyes and threw the covers off her body.

"Finn, let me find my socks."

Teenie stepped onto the parquet floor, grabbing her socks and jeans from the corner of the room, where she had thrown them the night before.

"Hurry, Teenie, I don't think I am going to make it," he said, holding himself.

"Shush, Finn," she whispered in his ear, "we may wake Delaney. Let's be quiet."

They walked past their sister Delaney, who was sound asleep in the twin bed on the other side of the room. She fell asleep wearing her favorite barbie doll.

Teenie looked down the hall and saw a sliver of light peeking through the crack at the bottom of the bathroom door.

Oh no, thought Teenie, someone is inside.

She pounded on the door.

"I'm in here," yelled Shamus, their older brother.

"Finn has to pee, so get out. You've been in there longer than ten minutes," she lied.

Teenie referred to the sign hanging on the door by a thumbtack that stated, *10 MINUTES AND OUT.*

"Get lost, Teenie, I just got in here," Shamus yelled.

Teenie asked Finn, who was standing next to her, "do you want to go down to the other toilet?"

Teenie was referring to the other toilet, the one no one uses. It sits in the center of the cellar, where it is dark and creepy.

"I'm scared. I don't like to go to that potty," replies Finn.

"It's fine; I'll take you down."

Teenie takes Finn's tiny hand and heads downstairs. s they round the kitchen, Teeney remembers the pee-pee jar stored under the kitchen sink. She asked Finn if he wanted to use it.

"No pee-pee jar Teenie. I'm a big boy now," he says.

They head to the cellar door. Teenie reaches for the cellar doorknob, and it sticks. She gives it a good pull. The dankness of the basement hit both Finn and Tennie in the face.

"I don't like this smell," Finn says.

"It's just the musty floor, she said.

Teenie flips on the wall switch, which barely illuminates the staircase.

Finn held onto the railing as they slowly went down the narrow steps. He takes one step at a time, tightly squeezing her hand. She could feel his nervousness.

"Teenie, see, I'm a big boy, and I am not scared of the basement."

"You are such a big boy," Teenie says.

They reached the bottom step entering more darkness.

"Finn, stay on this step while Teenie puts on the overhead light by the toilet."

Teenie trots on the balls of her feet and reaches up to pull the chain. The lightbulb is covered in cobwebs which gives her the creeps.

"Hurry, Teenie," Finn cries. "Hold me."

Teenie carries him a few steps to the toilet. The toilet has rust stains from lack of use.

There are baskets of dirty laundry stacked by the washer and dryer, piles of magazines, bikes, chairs, old coolers, dusty silk flower arrangements, and boxes filled with miscellaneous items crowd the basement floor. The ping pong table was covered with clean clothing. Mom uses the table to fold clothes that are overflowing with unmatched socks.

"You ready, Finn?"

"Thanks, Teenie. I feel much better."

Finn and Teenie walked up the steps into the kitchen, finding their mom at the kitchen table drinking her morning coffee, looking as though she had very little sleep last night.

Patrick and Conor sat across from her, shoveling cereal into their mouths, with their heads bent down.

These two little partners in crime must have just gotten out of bed.

"Hey, Ma, how are you feeling, asked Teenie."

"Not good this morning Teenie, get Finn his breakfast, sweetie, will ya?" She toasted Finn a waffle, added butter and maple syrup, and handed him his favorite fork.

"Mom, Finn's curls are matted to the back of his head today. Please ask Delaney to use the magic lotion and comb them out."

Finn quickly looks up from his plate and says, "Nope."

"I'll handle Finn this morning, don't worry yourself, Teenie."

I head upstairs to get dressed.

I brush my teeth and hair, put on my jeans and Tee Shirt, pushing her curly hair back in a headband. I love this tee-shirt, she said out loud to herself. It has a washed-out peace sign on it. Next, she looked for her flip-flops but could only find one. I bet my sister, Delaney, wore them, and now I can only find one, she grumbled. Finally, she put on her clogs and headed out.

Chapter Two
The Goberts

It is early Monday morning and, the heat is sizzling off the streets. I shield my eyes from the blaring sun. It is trash day, and the stench from the overflowing trash cans is almost too much to endure.

Oh, for the love of all things holy, Crazy Eddie is standing on the corner. I cross the street so I can ignore him. Crazy Eddie is an older man who I heard chases kids with knives. I never saw it with my own eyes, but I believe it. My best friend, Cindy, listened to the same stories, so it must be true.

I try to pretend he doesn't exist and make no eye contact. If he comes at me with a knife, I figure I can run fast, and he will never catch me. I hope he doesn't chase me because I don't want to get to the Goberts any sooner than I have to.

As I round the corner, I see Mrs. Bodine sweeping the sidewalk. "Good morning, Teenie," she says. "How is your momma feeling?"

Not so well this morning; her iron is low, so she gets tired." Mrs. Bodine has raised eight children; she knows well how tired my mom is.

"Well, you tell your momma if she needs anything, just give me a shout. I'll stop around to see her real soon."

I thank her and move on.

Checking my watch, I have ten more minutes before entering the craziness of the Gobert house. I slow my pace, studying the cracks in the sidewalk. I attempt to identify any animal shapes as I walk along. It's a mind game I always play.

It is early in the summer, and I regret my decision to babysit the Gobert children. Mom says I should be thankful for the job opportunity this summer, but I am not feeling so lucky. The Gobert house is different this year and not in a good way.

Tim and Teresa Gobert have three children, Penelope is nine, Emma is eight, and Little Frannie is five.

They are such beautiful children. Penelope has gorgeous strawberry blond hair with deep brown eyes. Her eyes are so dark, and they appear black. Emma is also pretty with the same beautiful hair and hazel eyes. She has a slight overbite with deep dimples. Little Frannie has thick dark hair and the same deep brown eyes as Penelope.

I arrive at the Goberts and pull open the screen door, which is hanging from the hinges. Penelope and Kathleen are the only ones awake this morning, and they look relieved to see me.

"Good morning girls, did you eat breakfast yet?"

They both start talking at the same time. "Teenie, my mommy, left early this morning, right after daddy, and there is no milk in the refrigerator. I wanted to pour cereal for Kathleen and me, but we don't want to eat dry cereal again."

"It's okay, Penelope," I say.

I open the refrigerator, and I know it's another day to figure out what to feed the kids. The fridge is dirty, filled with Styrofoam food containers gone stale. There is a bottle of unopened apple juice which I feel more thankful for than I should.

I asked Mr. Gobert when he arrived home on Friday if they were going food shopping over the weekend. He mentioned they would be doing a food order but needed to check with Mrs. Gobert about which day. He did apologize for the lack of food. He said things have been so hectic. Mrs. Gobert's work hours at the law firm have increased, and they are behind in household chores. I let him know I hung a food list, with a plastic alphabet magnet, on the refrigerator, for the children. I'm guessing their weekend was too busy to think of food.

It seems there isn't much to eat in the house since I started at the beginning of June. Last summer, the cupboards were always full, and it was rare to run out of milk.

I would like to talk to Mrs. Gobert about the food shortage, but I rarely see her. She is never here when I arrive or leave.

I checked the cupboard, and there was a quarter loaf of white bread and peanut butter on the shelf. I will make slices of peanut butter toast for them this morning.

This job is like running a marathon in concrete boots.

◆

 New to writing, Mary Ann Barry is focused on humorous non-fiction. She was born and raised in Philadelphia and now lives in southern New Jersey. She came to and participates in DWG through our online meetings. This piece was mentored by experienced members of the group.

DWG

PATRICIA POLLACK

Emergency Department – May I help You?

It was 6 a.m. in the emergency department, and unit secretary Becky Rowan was deep into her end-of-shift cleaning ritual of wiping down her workstation with a cloth and antiseptic spray. She would flush out the dust bunnies hiding behind the computer and underneath the telephone. It was a satisfying process, and yet disgusting, when a cloud of dead skin cells, hair and food remnants go airborne, which is why she always held her breath.

"Becky, I'd be careful cleaning the phone," warned Gwen Wilcox, her fellow unit secretary and friend of six years. "You will wake it from its sleep."

"See that?" Gwen pointed. "The phone is silent. The clear buttons are unlit. There are no incoming calls, and I want to keep it that way. We go home soon."

Becky smirked. She was superstitious too. But she was willing to roll the dice. She folded her cloth in half and in half again. With the last fold completed, the cloth was in the shape of a triangle. She pinched one of the triangular points until it resembled a sharp instrument and cautiously aimed it toward the phone, moving in like a specialist defusing a bomb.

But it was too late. Line one woke up.

The women stared at each other, surprised and yet not surprised.

"I got it," moaned Gwen, picking up the call from her side of the workstation. "Emergency Department, may I help you?"

Gwen listened intently then said, "Hold please, while I get a physician."

She flashed an "I told you so" look at Becky, pressed the button on the phone that said overhead speaker and began talking.

"Medical commander needed on line one. We need a physician to pick up line one for a class-one medical," echoed her voice throughout the department.

"I got this, Gwen," said Dr. Dobson carrying a hot cup of coffee back from the staff lounge. He knew medical commander meant a paramedic was requesting physician assistance on a critical patient. Dr. Dobson pressed his lips against the Styrofoam cup, then took a slow slurp for some high-octane energy before picking up the receiver.

"This is Dr. Dobson, medical commander. Go ahead." Dr. Dobson was a 56-year-old fixture in the department. An *aw-shucks* kind of guy with sandy brown hair and a wrinkled lab coat that had not seen the inside of a washing machine in months.

He reached for the required paper, then pushed his crooked glasses back up on his nose, preparing to take the report.

Third-year emergency resident Dr. Kate Gelston was surrounded by a cluster of nurses, secretaries, and physicians all drawn to the call like moths to a flame. They listened to the crackling sound of a medic giving a radio report from the back of an ambulance.

"This is Medic Mike Lancing. We are less than four minutes out with a 30-year-old female in cardiac respiratory arrest. How do you copy?"

"I copy," said Dr. Dobson, looking up at the crowd gathering before him. They were the faces of exhausted people with droopy eyelids, who had been on duty almost 11 hours and only minutes earlier had been dreaming of going home to bed.

"Patient was found unresponsive by her husband at 5:30 this morning. She has no palpable pulse, absent heart sounds, not breathing on her own. Oxygen is being delivered via bag-valve mask. CPR is in progress," he said in one breath, trying to remain calm. But a clinically-dead young woman rattles everyone.

"No pulse, no respirations," affirmed Dr. Dobson. "Continue with CPR. Hey Mike, did you say she is intubated?" he asked, referring to the placement of a breathing tube into the patient's trachea.

"No, not intubated, too much vomit in her airway. We tried, had one failed attempt. So, we're delivering oxygen through a mask. Our estimated time of arrival is two minutes. I'll give you the rest of report when I see you."

"Got it. Dobson out."

"Are you going to run this case?" Dobson asked Dr. Kate. "I'll be in the room if you need anything."

"Absolutely, I want the experience." she insisted.

Dr. Kate was at the end of her emergency medicine residency. Graduation day was only months away. She had already accepted a position at a small community hospital in Burlington, Vermont, where she would be the only emergency physician on duty.

"We have an arrest coming in. We're going to need nursing and a respiratory therapist," she told the group. "And Gwen?" she shouted. "Call for the portable chest x-ray."

It was nurse Melissa Miller's slender finger that flipped on the light switch, illuminating the stark clinical exam room with a hospital stretcher placed strategically in the center. The crisp white sheet that fit tightly over the mattress was stripped off and replaced with a blue body bag. A new sheet was placed on top as if nothing were odd.

The true purpose of a hard mattress eludes most patients. It's not meant to make patients uncomfortable; it serves as a firm surface to help maximize the force of a chest compression during CPR, effectively sandwiching one's chest between the two forces.

To the left of the stretcher sat a five-drawer code cart with a cardiac defibrator resting on top, always ready to deliver electrical shocks when energized.

Crossing the threshold one by one arrived the regulars: Charge Nurse Beth, Respiratory Therapist Tony, Nurse Ann, and her student Lincoln Powell, joining Dr. Dobson and Dr. Kate.

"Do you mind if my student Lincoln stays in the room? He's a smart guy, wants to go into emergency nursing." said Nurse Ann to Nurse Melissa as they gathered the syringes, intravenous (IV) fluids, and tubing in preparation for the patient. "He ran on an ambulance. Only did CPR twice."

"Lincoln?" repeated Nurse Melissa, wondering what a modern-day Lincoln would look like. She scanned the room, looking for the unfamiliar face. Lincoln occupied a football player's body, stood well over six feet with biceps and pecks that stretched out his scrub shirt like it was one size too small.

"He can stay," winked Nurse Melissa. "He's easy on the eyes." She remembered being a student herself and was sensitive to the pressures of learning. "Ann, you're going to stick around and help, right? This is going to be a tough case."

"Of course," she replied, then turned toward Lincoln. "Hey kid," she shouted over the growing chatter filling the room. "Do you want to do CPR?"

Lincoln's eyes widen. He pointed toward himself and croaked "Me?" His terror apparent despite his experience and daunting physique, he appeared frozen in place.

Nurse Melissa stepped closer to reassure him. "We're gonna tell you exactly what to do and when to do it. You heard of the Bee Gees song "Stayin' Alive," right? Well, use the words and the rhythm of that song to keep time for the chest compressions. Remember to push hard and fast. *Ah, Ah, Ah, Ah, stayin' alive, stayin' alive. Ah, Ah,* Got it?"

Lincoln nodded, the irony of the song not lost on him.

She continued, "In about one minute the paramedics will be coming through these exam doors and giving a report to the physicians. They're already doing CPR on the woman, so clinically she's dead. Our goal is to get her back from the dead."

Dr. Kate listened to Nurse Melissa's instructions while readying the airway equipment that would be inserted into the patient's throat. She was recalling all the years of training and teaching poured into her career, seemingly culminating into moments like this one. She would need to draw on that strength and more, right down to her starched lab coat and her string of white pearls she wore daily, channeling her hero, Barbara Bush.

"Quiet everyone. The medics are here," ordered Dr. Kate.

The patient arrived in the room headfirst. Her long and wavy brown hair covered the top half of the stretcher and spilled down the sides. Her face was completely obscured by the oxygen mask pressed firmly against her nose and mouth by Medic Mike, who delivered rhythmic puffs of oxygen every five seconds. His partner, riding on top of the stretcher, was perched above the patient, delivering CPR with outstretched hands that covered both her sternum and her left breast. She had chosen to wear a blue silky pajama top with matching shorts earlier in the evening that surely would have complimented her long slender legs and painted blue toenails.

"This is Melanie Williams," said Medic Mike, wiping the sweat from his forehead and off the tip of his nose. "She is a 30-year-old female in cardiac and respiratory arrest. She was last seen awake around 9 p.m. by her husband, who reports she complained of a frontal headache that began earlier in the day. He gave her two Percocet that he found in the back of their medicine cabinet and escorted her to bed."

Medic Mike paused while the team aligned the ambulance stretcher next to the emergency stretcher for the transfer of the patient. Lincoln waited for the okay from Nurse Ann, then stepped up on a stool to take over the chest compressions. He pushed down hard and fast.

"The husband says he fell asleep on the couch," Medic Mike continued. "When he checked on her this morning, she wasn't breathing."

"Did you know there is blood and vomit in her mouth?" asked Dr. Kate, rapidly turning the patient's head to the side and grabbing the suctioning wand to perform a sweeping action and clear the secretions from the pharynx.

"Yeah," said Medic Mike. "She was like that when we first saw her. We suctioned her several times on the way here. Husband says she has a past medical history of seizures. Maybe that's why she vomited. Bit her tongue. She takes 300-mg Dilantin three times daily."

To Dr. Kate's horror, secretions from the patient's stomach kept bubbling up into the throat. The only way to successfully intubate a patient is to get a clear view of the vocal cords then pass the tube between them and into the trachea. Her plan was to have Respiratory Tony suction the airway, and she would immediately attempt an intubation, which was exactly what happened.

She clasped the laryngoscope tightly in her left hand, inserted the curved metal blade deep into the patient's throat, and pulled upward, bringing the jaw forward until she could visualize the vocal cords, then slipped the tube between them and into the trachea. She could feel the tension in the room. It wasn't until Respiratory Tony confirmed the breathing tube was in the right place for oxygen to be effectively delivered that Dr. Kate exhaled loudly.

"Continue CPR," she ordered. Medic Mike resumed his report. "Her family doctor is Lawrence Schenker, Brighton Medical Center out on Route 80. Husband is on his way here. They have a daughter, named Ava. She's four years old."

Dr. Kate waited for several more rounds of CPR before stopping Lincoln. She looked at the unchanged monitor, placed her stethoscope on the patient's heart, listened for a beat, and shook her head no. Undaunted, she ordered the team to continue CPR and for Nurse Melissa to inject another syringe of epinephrine through the IV catheter. With each failed effort, the mood in the room turned more somber.

"Let's try shocking at 360 Joules, the maximum," Dr. Kate ordered.

Nurse Melissa tapped Lincoln on his arm, motioning for him to stop CPR. Nurse Ann placed the defibrillator pads onto the patient's chest.

"Lincoln," said Nurse Melissa, pointing to the cardiac monitor. "You see that flat line? That means there is no electrical activity in the heart. It's completely still. No electrical impulse to stimulate the heart muscle to squeeze and make it pump blood forward. But Dr. Kate is hoping, despite all the odds and what we are seeing, that a weak electrical current could be present. The patient is young, so we're gonna shock her, pray we restore a normal rhythm, and let her heart beat again."

"Excuse me, excuse me, Dr Dobson!" interrupted Pastor Mary with a sense of urgency. She was standing outside the exam room peeking in from behind the curtain. "I have the patient's husband right here. Can he come in?"

"Mary, please, not now," Dr. Dobson said. Dr. Kate knew Dr. Dobson was protecting her from the husband's intense emotions, possible scrutiny, but it wasn't necessary. She could handle it.

"Bring him in," said Dr. Kate, overriding his order, then nodding for Nurse Ann to begin.

"Charging. Everyone stand back," Nurse Ann shouted. She waited for the ear-piercing tone to reach its peak, then depressed the buttons that delivered the electrical shock directly into the heart.

The jolt caused every muscle in the patient's body to lurch upward, seemingly lifting her off the mattress. But it had no effect on a flaccid heart.

"Continue CPR," Dr. Kate ordered. She knew it was futile, but now it was Dr. Kate who was protecting the husband.

She reached down to lightly touch the patient's skin, but it was already becoming cold. She slipped her hand into her pocket, pulled out her pen light, and shined it into lifeless pupils, both fixed and dilated.

It was over for everyone but the husband. Hope was the last thing to die. Dr. Kate walked toward him, realizing she didn't know his first or last name. He had stood watching in the corner of the room in stunned silence. She would be part of a defining moment. He would retell this story of his wife's headache, her lifeless body, the pungent smell of vomit in her hair, the dried trickle of blood between her fingers and around her wedding band for all eternity.

"I'm Dr. Kate Gelston," she uttered softly, feeling instead like he was hearing her say, I'm Dr. Death. "I am so sorry. We did everything we could to save her life. But nothing has worked."

He stared directly at the body of his wife, then moved his gaze into the eyes of Dr. Kate, searching for answers. "She has had CPR for over 40 minutes. We have given her a total of four syringes of epinephrine and we tried shocking her heart. Nothing has worked. She is dead. I think it's time to stop."

He looked at the team of doctors and nurses standing at the bedside watching Student Nurse Lincoln and Respiratory Tony continue to deliver oxygen and chest compressions. It was clear; all eyes were upon him awaiting his decision.

He said nothing, then burst into tears. "I'm sorry. I'm so sorry. I didn't mean to …"

Dr. Dobson and Dr. Kate fixed their eyes upon each other. They knew this case just got a lot more complicated after that statement. They politely excused themselves and headed toward the desk of the unit secretary.

"Dr. Dobson," asked Becky. "Should I call her family doctor to come in and sign the death certificate?"

"No."

Dr. Dobson looked at Dr. Kate, ran his fingers through his hair, and scratched his head. "I don't know why this woman is dead. I don't know the manner or the cause. There are just too many unknowns."

He turned toward Becky, leaned over the desk, and gave an order.

"Get the coroner on the phone."

Patricia has a bachelor's degree in journalism from Rowan University, NJ. She worked as a newspaper reporter at the Courier Post serving South Jersey and the editor of the WellSpan Hospital Nursing Newsletter in York, PA. Patricia was an emergency and trauma nurse for many years. She earned a Master of Science in nursing education from University of South Florida. She is currently adjunct faculty at Jefferson College of Nursing in Philadelphia. Patricia lives in Center City Philadelphia. PatriciaJPollack@Yahoo.com.

DWG

GAYLE SIMMONS

Some Things Never Change

Nick is on the way out the door as I stroll into the kitchen. "Good morning, Chickie. Sleep well?" he says. "I'm headed to the post office, and thought I'd take your car to the carwash. If you need it in the next hour or so, I won't bother, but it's pretty disgusting. I don't want to take my truck to the reunion tonight. They'll think we're ready to apply for welfare."

Before Nick, my husband for over nine years, I never had a pet name, not even from my parents. I don't recall when Nick bequeathed this nickname to me. *Chickie*—it's unique. Better than the generic *hon* or *sugar*.

"I know this is last minute, Nick, but would you mind terribly if I passed on tonight? It's the end of the marking period, I'm swamped with papers to grade before Monday, and I'm not in the mood for Emily's prattle."

"Of course, I'd mind. C'mon, Claire. You can tolerate her for one evening, can't you? Your friends are expecting you and I'd be disappointed if you don't come. It's a ten-year event."

"Sorry. You're right. I'll be in a better mood after my shower. Take the car. I'm certainly not going anywhere."

I grade papers at my desk upstairs. Before I realize the passing time, Nick calls from the kitchen.

"Anyone home?"

"I'm still working on the exams, not close to being finished."

"Take your time. I'll grab something to eat. Would you like something?"

"I definitely need a break. Blueberry yogurt with a handful of fresh ones thrown in sounds delicious. Thanks. I'll be down in a minute."

While I'm in the shower, Nick peeks his head into the bathroom.

"Claire, how dressed up are you getting for tonight?"

"Not very," I shout over the running water. "What about you?"

"I was thinking about the blue shirt you gave me for my birthday and a sport jacket, but no tie since this isn't a dressy group. How's that sound?"

"Fine. I'm wearing my usual black dress. Hope you don't mind because you've seen it so many times. You know how I loathe shopping."

"The black dress is perfect. We should leave by 5:30 because *hors' d'oeuvres* and drinks are being served from 6:00 to 7:00 before dinner. I'll have to park the car in the lot, so that should give us plenty of time."

"I'll be ready."

"Oh, I forgot to tell you. Andrew texted me to say that Cam is coming from Colorado. Evidently, Bryce contacted him then Bryce told Andrew and Andrew told me. The chain of command. Are you comfortable with this?"

"Cameron's coming?"

"Yep, all the way from the old West. Are you ready for that?"

"Uh … well … sure. Absolutely! Why wouldn't I be? That was ancient history, and you know I was over him years ago. Can this wait? I can barely hear you over the shower!"

"Sorry, I only wanted to be sure you're okay with seeing him again. That's all. I know it's been a long time."

"I am quite comfortable," I shout over the cascading water.

Stepping out of the shower, I almost trip over the low ledge. I can't believe Cameron is coming. The news catches me off guard. Whenever Cam's name comes up, I do my best to change the conversation. After gaining my balance and sanity, I comb through my long, tangled hair followed by a quick drying.

Late that afternoon, putting on my face takes only a few minutes with mascara and eyeliner to set off my blue eyes, a bit of blush, some pale pink lipstick, and a fine spray of my favorite scent, *Euphoria,* by Calvin Klein, which I've used since college. Will Cam recognize it?

"My God, Claire, you look fantastic," Nick says. "The dress may not be new, but it's spot on, shows off your loveliness. You don't look a year older than when we met on Nantucket. I'm sure your blond, silky hair is envied by many women."

"Thanks, Nick, but I doubt I look the same. I'm a little wobbly in these high sandals. Maybe I shouldn't wear them, don't want to make a grand entrance by falling on my face."

"Hey, since we're a little early would you like me to pop the bottle of bubbly to celebrate the occasion? Since it was a school night, we never opened it on your birthday."

In need of support I answer, "That sounds great. We'll get a head start on the party."

He goes into the kitchen and returns with two flutes of champagne.

"Thanks for changing your mind about tonight. Here's looking at you, kid." The final scene in *Casablanca* with Bogart and Bergman is Nick's favorite toast.

"And, here's to you."

After two glasses each, we head off to The Hyatt at Boston Harbor, only a ten-minute drive.

It's the tenth reunion of Boston graduates of Dartmouth College. Nick graciously drops me off in front of the stately hotel while he parks the Volvo in the lot. I quickly run a comb through my hair and freshen my lipstick.

While waiting for Nick, trepidation sets in. Why has Cameron always made me behave like a school girl? Nick strides around the corner looking quite pleased with himself.

"Here we are, Chickie. Let's go in and get this party started. You look so beautiful I can't wait to show you off."

"Nick, I'm nervous."

"Relax, everything will be fine. C'mon, let's go. Our friends are waiting."

This time with the familiar refrain, *everything will be fine*, he has no idea what he's talking about.

The gathering is set up on a large, covered patio with torch lighting, ample tables covered in linens, comfortable chairs, an extensive bar, and a lavish display of hors d'oeuvres: a seasonal crudité platter, baked and raw clams, cheese tray, stuffed mushrooms and shrimp cocktail.

After a profusion of hugs, kisses and friendly conversations, I'm able to step off to the side to scan the crowded patio. Cam should be here by now. Would he have vetoed the trip? A drink will help calm my nerves. Oh, no, here come the Smiths just as I was about to say hi to Bryce. I thought he might say something about Cam.

"Hi, Emily. Hi, Andrew," I say. "It's been too long. How have you been? I'm sure you're busy with the business and your family."

Andrew pulls Nick off to the side for some manly talk.

"I'm so happy to see you, Claire," Emily starts. "We're both fine and, yes, very busy with the kids now that they're out of school for the summer, but it's fun. The insurance business is running smoothly, and making us oodles of money. Have you heard Andrew and I are planning a trip to New Zealand in August, without the kids? We can't wait. You're looking gorgeous as usual."

"Sounds wonderful. Nick's not big on long distance traveling."

They move on. Hope I wasn't too abrupt. Now's my chance to break away.

"Nick, go over and say hi to Bryce. He's munching hors d'oeuvres and trying to catch your eye. I'm going to the bar for a glass of wine. Would you like anything?"

"No thanks. I got a beer earlier. Be careful, Chickie, don't let some handsome man whisk you away."

If he only knew. Now, where are you, Cam?

"A white wine spritzer, please, lots of ice. Thank you."

When my drink arrives, I take a few tentative sips, remembering there's still champagne in my system. Sitting alone I realize if he doesn't show, there's not a damn thing I can do about it other than be desperately disappointed.

Then, I feel a light tap on my shoulder. I slowly swivel my bar stool around. There he is … in a blue striped shirt and khakis, handsome as always. Even though I'm sitting, my legs feel weak, and for a second, I'm speechless.

"Oh, my God, you're here. When I didn't see you, I was afraid you changed your mind. Uh, what would you like to drink? Let me look at you."

"How 'bout if we look at each other? You look wonderful, Claire, which is no surprise. There wasn't a doubt I would recognize you. Your hair is much longer, I like it. But that fragrance is familiar."

He orders a Corona with lime.

"You look wonderful yourself," I say. "Making good use of your gym membership. And the tortoise shell glasses look great on you. How are you? How was your flight, where are you staying, how's Jane?"

"Slow down, Claire. Take a breath. Too many questions, too fast. Yes, I frequent the gym, traded in the old wire frames, the flight was uneventful, I'm staying at the Residence Inn at the airport. Jane is fine, busy at work as usual, and I'm well . . . especially now. Damn, it's good to see you! But I have to admit I'm having trouble processing that you're sitting here beside me. Five years is too fuckin' long. Sorry for the language."

He gives me that same grin that tells me he's not at all sorry.

"Sorry, about blurting out all the questions. Guess I'm a little nervous."

A distinct tingling runs up my arm as he places his hand over mine. A gesture to calm my nerves. Nick is across the room talking to Zach, his best friend from Dartmouth. It's good to see Nick happy, and I'm relieved he's not facing my way.

"We don't want anyone getting ideas, Cam. Even though we have a history, I'm sure the gossip is no longer interesting. But you never know when old news can resurface. Besides, you want to visit with your friends. It's been a long time for them also. Don't let me hold you captive."

What am I saying? That's exactly what I want to do.

"Not so fast," he says. "Who cares if someone notices us? We're just friends catching up like they are. This is quite a place. Seems a little classy for this gang."

"That's what Nick and I thought. Andrew was in charge of booking, and I'm sure his wife Emily played a part."

The last spritzer gives me the courage to ask, "Do you have an early morning flight?" Please, God, let him say no.

"Glad you asked. I'm not leaving until Monday morning at seven, was hoping we might be able to spend some time together without feeling like our friends are peering over our shoulders. I don't mean that unkindly. May I be honest, Claire?"

"Haven't you always been?"

"Well then, I must tell you something."

"Well then, go ahead."

He leans close to my ear.

"I'm only here, Claire, to see you."

My God, I can't believe what I'm hearing. He wants to get together.

"And the only reason *I'm* here," I answer, looking deeply into his blue eyes, "is to see you."

He backs off slightly with that grin.

"I almost stayed home," I say.

"What? Why?"

"Because I didn't know you were coming until this afternoon. Yes, I'd love to spend time with you. It's a rare opportunity. What do you have in mind?"

Am I imagining the same old chemistry between us? But the warmth coursing through my body is not my imagination. Perhaps it's true that some things never change.

"Was I too forward," he says, "by asking to spend time with you tomorrow. Sitting here with you makes me realize how much I've missed you. Remember five years ago at the harbor when you placed a heart-shaped stone in my hand before you drove off? It's been on my writing desk ever since."

"I remember. It was a spring day, and we took a walk along the water, holding hands. I've often wondered if I did the right thing by giving the stone to you with no explanation. I'm happy you still have it. And don't be silly, you can never be too forward with me."

I don't tell him that the stone represents my love for him, but knowing our telepathy, I'm sure he understands.

"Can you spare a few hours?" he asks. "We can go out for breakfast or lunch if you like. Do you know the Residence Inn at the airport? I think it's fairly new."

"Nick and I were at a wedding reception at the Inn last month. And I have no plans tomorrow so, if you like, we can make it a day rather than a few hours."

"A whole day? Perfect. What time is good for you? Remember, tonight may go late."

"Gosh, I don't know. "How 'bout … ten?"

"Ten it is," he agrees.

"They're calling for rain, so instead of going out, why don't I bring coffee—cream for you, right? There's a great coffee and bagel shop in the shopping center right next to the Inn."

"Excellent idea. If anything unforeseen comes up, like bursting water pipes, give me a call, and we'll make alternate plans. I can come and throw a rescue line to you. Otherwise, I'm in room 123."

There's that wit I love. He eyes me curiously, like he's wondering what's going on when I suggested not going out for breakfast. If he only knew, but … surely, he does. I don't tell him Nick has to work all day tomorrow, which works perfectly with Cam's invitation.

"Sounds like we have a plan," he says. I'll find you later to say goodnight."

"You better. Nick would like to say hi. Surprisingly, he was happy you were joining us tonight. He's over by the hors d'oeuvres talking with Zach."

"Is he still sensitive about us?"

"Mmmm, a little, but it's okay. Go talk to him."

It's not easy letting him go.

He takes my hand again.

"I have to admit I was nervous on the plane. A lot can change over time, but I don't feel any changes here. So, it looks like we have a 10:00 date tomorrow morning. Don't forget."

Is he kidding!!

"There's so much I want to ask you, Cam. Can't wait to hear about your latest book. I sent you an e-mail about how much I loved the Bermuda novel. Did you see my review? We'll talk more about everything tomorrow. I agree talking too long here is kind of awkward. See you soon."

He gave my upper arm a firm squeeze. "Claire, I am so happy you came."

"And I would never have forgiven myself if I didn't. Okay then, until tomorrow, coffee with cream and bagels. Sounds like fun. Now go mingle."

As he walks away from the bar, there's a flaming sensation in my core. My body is rushing down a path I know I shouldn't follow, but there's no control, no recalling the last time for this feeling, but I welcome it with open arms, mind and heart. The rest of the evening passes in a blur, my mind is only on tomorrow.

 Gayle Simmons received her undergraduate degree from Penn State University and a Master's Degree in Education from Stony Brook University Southampton, New York. She currently lives and teaches high school English in Lititz, PA (Lancaster County). She has been able to take advantage of DWG's meetings and recordings on Zoom. This is her first published narrative.

DW**G**

MICHAEL MARRA

It Is Finished

The following is an excerpt from Book Three of the trilogy that began with Ghost – Where Truth and Fiction Collide *and was followed by* Made in America. *Based on true crime, the content is graphic and brutal. The language is laced with vulgarity and violence which lends to the authenticity of the time.*

The puddle of blood beneath his head continued to pool. His right arm was broken, and his left leg fractured. At least four inches of the tibia were exposed. There was not one tooth visible in his mouth. His face had been beaten severely. I remember hearing a gunshot as I stood to leave. The top of his skull was blown away. There was no recollection of me firing a shot, yet my holster was unmetered. An ice pick was in his left eye driven into its hilt, a wooden handle. I didn't carry an ice pick! My weapon was fired because there was a spent round in the chamber.

The only thing I remember clearly was the initial encounter and my confrontation with him which I dominated. But now, walking away, all I could see was the red snow. Six inches had fallen here in New York City. I have seen many dead bodies and this man, who was named Mazzini, was one of them.

When I got the chance and was sure to be out of the sight of unwanted eyes, I washed up thoroughly with the freshly fallen snow. There was an odd pinching like feeling in the side of my abdomen, but I felt no blood and would check it out later. When I saw the amount of blood in the snow that was just from washing up, it was unnerving. I moved to another spot of fresh snow, knelt again and washed some more.

I would have to see Zio before I went home to Tracy. What in the hell happened? Did I kill Mazzini? Something was missing. I never allowed myself to become that enraged to blackout. Keeping my focus is what I was taught. Every move was deliberate. This was completely out of character for me. Something was wrong!

Yes, I said I had wanted him dead and to pay for all he had done. First, he shot me. He abducted Tracy and her mother. He put the word on the street that there was a bounty offered for my whereabouts. Those were all big mistakes which had already put eyes on him. Yeah, he was a made man but when an approval is given, and the order goes out from a boss, your time is short. Otherwise, taking out a made man is not done. Beyond that, he did harm to another family and, without approval, took out a made man. These are all things punishable by death. Why don't I remember blowing his skull to pieces?

I had found his whereabouts through hearing of his habits and how he began his day. He knew there was a target on him, which made me wonder why he hadn't changed up his routine. Stalking him, I decided on the most secure place to confront him. It was a secluded alley and he had exited the only side door of the club. My intention was to beat him man to man with my fists and only use a weapon if there was no choice. That is how I would gain my satisfaction. He was of the mind that he could not be taken out hand to hand. After all, the man was huge at six foot seven and a muscular two hundred eighty pounds. He was feared by most, but he had crossed the line. The imposing figure he presented to most exuded fear. For me, it was exhilarating. It made me stronger.

When there is a vengeance brewing that has come to a boil there is no fear on my part. Only the objective. Mazzini was even given a fair shot as we stood face to face. It would have been easy to blindside him, but there would be no satisfaction in that. We locked eyes after I lit a Lucky and snapped the Zippo closed. Yes, dented from his bullet, it was the same one that had saved my life. The only thing he had time to do was smirk. When I walked away there was no smirk, only a battered body in red snow.

The Staple Street bridge was above me as I walked. Ironically, it was where Mazzini had pulled the trigger twice to end me. His bullets found their mark, but not enough to take me out. Now, I was aware as the black Lincoln Town car that pulled alongside me and stopped. The second time I had seen it. It was a moment for decisive action. This alley had almost claimed me once. It would not succeed this time. I heard a voice that relieved any anxiety while I reached for my .357.

"Hey, Luca, c'mon, get in. Let's get outta here!" It was Tommy "Chiclets," who was a steadfast figure in my life. Not only was he Zio's number one man that never left his side, he watched out for me as well. Zio had other trusted men but Tommy was number one, which made this encounter even more surprising. So it was that the car I had spotted was the car I was now in. Why was the rest a blur? I kept going back to the fury in which I unleashed my rage that was the reason Mazzini was dead.

"Have you had eyes on me Tommy?" If he said yes, I would know that he couldn't have. Tommy would never bullshit me. In fact, it would be Mazzini he had eyes on. I happened to show up. I know there were no eyes on me! There were some orders that came down regarding Mazzini and maybe Tommy and some of the crew were there to take care of business. Regardless of what it was, I know what it is. Mazzini is dead. My weapon was fired, and I am a bloody mess, none of it mine but bloody, nonetheless.

"Luca, geez we gotta' get you cleaned up! You got blood all over you!"

"I washed up in the snow, Tommy." I was lightheaded but it was euphoric like a high.

"It's all over your clothes and your gloves and your hair. To answer your question, yes, we were looking for Mazzini. But you don't think I'm surprised to find you here, do you?"

"I thought I cleaned up pretty good, but I lost it a little at the end. Tommy, I don't remember shootin' the motherfucker! What's goin' on? Sorry about the car."

"Christ, you are losing it, Luca. You're sittin' on fuckin' plastic! I'm going to' get you over to Zio."

It took about fifteen minutes to get to the restaurant and still I felt like I was high. I reasoned that all the adrenaline and the release of endorphins could have me feelin' this way. The car stopped at a side door of the restaurant.

"Luca, stai bene?" Luca are you okay. Zio's voice boomed from the back of the restaurant. *"Fatti vedere da."* Let me see you."

I walked toward his voice.

"Si, Zio sto bene." Yes, Zio, I'm fine.

He grimaced, not liking what he saw. I never wanted him to see me like this. He motioned for me to go to his office and clean up.

I went to his private office to take a shower. When I saw how much more blood spiraled down the drain, I was surprised. Zio arranged for almost an identical set of clothing I had been wearing. You could not take this man for granted! If you thought, he didn't know something, then think again.

For the first time, it was difficult to imagine our conversation, seeing where I had just come from. He was seated at his desk with his head down and his hands clasped together.

"Lei mie scuse. My apologies. Zio, I did not think it would come to this." I paused, unclasping his hands and motioning for me to continue.

"Yes, I was looking for him and I expressed that to you many times. I found him and took care of business."

Then Zio spoke from what appeared to be his own experience.

"I am not going to speak of how my men found this man. That is your business, and I will leave that to you. But I will tell you this, my son, things like this do not leave you. There may be demons you have to conquer, and it will help if you weigh what he has done to you to what you have taken from him. It is there you may find some comfort. The man shot you, Luca!"

Zio had eyes that could make you feel cold or comfort you. But now, they were angry eyes. Of course, I had heard some stories about Zio when he was younger, but nothing was ever validated. Yes, he was used for his brains and his street savvy, but it was his hands and intimidation that got him to be noticed quickly. It didn't hurt that the Don was like a second father to him.

"So, what happens next Zio? What about Mazzini?"

"Luca, Mazzini has not been seen for days. He went on vacation and he will not be returning. As for you, you have been dead and buried in Italy for several weeks now." I felt compelled to smile.

"But there are people that know who I am Zio. If they see me and say something?"

"And who are they going to say it to? People don't like it when the water goes above their nose. Anyone that knows you from the family will come to me with questions before anyone else." He put his hand like a salute just above his nose.

"I get it. The water," I answered. It bothered me that it took so long for me to grasp. If anyone saw me that was trusted they knew what the story was. I was murdered. If a rival or a rogue happened to spot me and say something, then maybe his shoes would get heavy and they would make him sink in the water.

Zio winked as if he saw the light bulb go on over my head.

"Listen carefully to me. For over three years you have been a made man. We both know how that happened and the reason it had to happen. Now, Luca, because you are a made man and the order was given to take out Mazzini, you carried that out. You had power before, but now you have a great deal of power."

"But I'm dead, Zio! What kind of power do I have?"

"You are only dead to the people that need to think that. The ones that need to know see you as a stand-up guy. This is a rare thing because it has never been done before. A made man and untouchable. A dead man yet you walk amongst us. Ombra, (shadow) is your name to us. You knew this was coming, Luca. Now, you have a beautiful life to live. You are almost done with these suits you are working for and we have benefited from that. You go home to your Tracy and get ready for your vacation and give me some great nieces and nephews!"

It would be his first. Zio did not have a great niece or nephew. Hey, I'm not sayin' I'm ready to get on that wagon. He knew that I would remain part of an elite circle for as long as I wanted. He also knew that I wanted a life that was not just Family. I was glad that I made good things happen for the Don and that I was in his favor. I could see in my memory what I thought was a frail older man when my grandfather introduced me to him as a little boy. I'd come to know that he was anything but frail and the most powerful man in the city if not the country.

I threw out the past and got immediately back to the present. I still wasn't satisfied with the way things went down with Mazzini. Yeah, he deserved to have his head blown off, but I don't recall it and I certainly don't remember any ice pick. It got me thinking about who was with Tommy "Chiclets" when I got in the car. It was Gianni 'Needles' Cardone. A big rotund man at about 250 pounds, he was surprisingly agile and was known for his expertise in putting people to sleep—a deep sleep that required a headstone. Gianni had begun medical school in Europe before moving to America to be amongst Family. There were many uses for his expertise, and as it turned out one of his victims was me. Now I was beginning to get the answers to questions that had been tormenting me.

I had been being watched because Zio knew I was hunting. No one could stop me. Mazzini would be the objective as long as he drew breath. Tommy was sent to tail me and keep tabs on me especially if I found Mazzini. So, he knew that should he find Mazzini, he might very well find me.

While I sat on Mazzini's broken body delivering blows to his head, Mazzini was not responding yet I continued. It was then that Gianni "Needles" administered a cocktail. Using the smallest gauge needle he had, which was a 26 gauge, he stuck me in the side with it. It is precisely why I lost all memory of pulling a trigger or using an ice pick. The ice pick was another killer's MO (*Modis Operandi*), which means simply the way things work.

As Tommy 'Chiclets' related the story to me, it now made sense and gave me some comfort. However, there was one big problem! My piece was now a murder weapon. Not for long. Tommy explained that two shots were fired and the one from my weapon was not the kill shot. Gianni did not want to be around when Tommy gave me the skinny. He knew of my temper.

"Tommy, I know every drug out there. What did he use?"

"He used a dose of Phenobarbital and another I can't even pronounce. Obviously, the perfect amount." Tommy grinned. It was unusual, and I was so enraged that I never saw Gianni sneak up behind me.

"Yeah, it made me *stunad* (stupid or having one's head in the clouds) for a moment or two. Just long enough for someone to finish Mazzini."

"Luca, c'mon, the guy was yours. He was done. Zio didn't want the blood on your hands. Even though your gloves were dripping with it."

Tommy would normally joke and make light of many gruesome situations, but this was too personal. There was no need to know who pulled the trigger. I only knew now that it wasn't me. My heart could now find its normal rhythm and I could breathe easier.

~

Tracy knew the life because she was not only born into it but ultimately became a pawn when Mazzini abducted her. There was no love lost even though she was the gentlest soul on Earth. Telling her what occurred would happen in time and I didn't want to have her relive anything as unsettling as this brutal exchange. Her life already tormented by this man with him having kidnapped her and her mother. I would find the right time.

Broken.

After Tracy's shocking departure from this world, there was one thing I didn't know if she'd been aware of. That was when the doctor had told me that it was much too early in the pregnancy to save the baby after Tracy was lost. A baby? Did she know? When was she going to tell me? The barrage of questions was fired at me like an automatic weapon.

I was broken. My war with God grew more intense. Everything that I was living for was gone. To finally settle down and enjoy a happy life was torn from me like wolves tearing at their prey's flesh. Done, I was going to be done with everything. No more suits. No undercover work in the bowels of corruption. It would be Tracy and I—and little did I know a baby—to settle down with away from the brutality that was my life.

There were the classic stages of grief that I was all too familiar with. They are shock and denial, pain and guilt, anger, depression and finally acceptance. I could always understand and reason with the first group. But acceptance? Not happening! I wanted vengeance, which was my natural reaction. But all I could do was weep until my soul was empty. How does someone die from an aneurysm at twenty-four?

Grief consumed me and my vengeance was a rage that no one would want to see. But who do I deliver this wrath to? There was no person. The only thing there was is an entity that most of the world believes in. They call him or her God. Well, if God is so pure, rewarding, comforting and all powerful, where is my solace? I have nothing but emptiness and a renewal of my war with God. No one could offer me the answer I sought. At least, not to my liking. Yes, I would have a new path in life. The problem was that path, like me, was empty.

I would wonder at times if this was a payback for the utterly reprehensible things, I was responsible for. Some would even call it evil. In the life, situations were thrown at me and there were encounters where I did not have a choice. It's called self-preservation. So how is it that an empath could do such things to people? The answer is simple. It is the never-ending battle between good and evil, the oldest battle on earth. In spite of the fact that I experienced delight in my battles and walked away exhilarated, there was always that conflict within that tormented me.

I can't expect anyone to understand this mindset because you cannot unless you have lived it. Sure, you can imagine it, but you can never know it. The most important lesson that one will often make in life is believing that they know someone. The reason that I know this to be a fact is that I watched people lose their lives because they thought they knew someone. I was called a Ghost, which is something I never believed in. But now, all I needed to see one was a mirror.

Michael Marra grew up in New York City in the sixties. As a Special Operative for the Attorney General and two state Senators, Michael was instrumental in exposing corruption during his years working the streets. He attended John Jay and Columbia along with other institutions that offered specialized training. Marra is the author of two short story collections, *A Host of Suspects* and *When Angels Cry*. He has also written autobiographical trilogy: *Made in America* and *Ghost: Where Truth and Fiction Collide*, and *It Is Finished*, tales of corruption that include a tender love story.

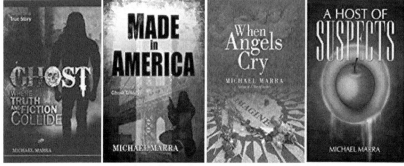

DWG

MARYANN HIGLEY HAMILTON

Bachelor of Arts

Coconut Grove, Florida
April, 1972

Yes, the address was right, but it didn't look like a frame shop. It didn't fit in with the eclectic mix of stores on Grand Avenue in the Grove. The display windows were filled with odds and ends from many years. Everything from a cow skull and a clam steamer in the right window, to antique furniture in the left window.

More in keeping with the Coconut Grove vibe was the art deco screen door with a slightly rusting pink palm tree design, that stood open. A weathered wood-and-glass front door was kept open by a large piece of coral.

A small sandy haired dog, wearing a plaid jacket with a pocket on the side stretched across the threshold enjoying the morning sun. Reluctantly he rose to let me enter the shop. The smell of pine and mineral spirits mingled with the salt air from nearby Biscayne Bay irritated my nose. Inside a tall slender man swept sandy dirt and leaves across the terrazzo floor towards the door.

"Mornin!" he greeted me in a light southern accent. "Have a seat, I'll be with you soon as I get rid of all this

277

mess. The wind we had this morning sure did stir things up in here." He paused, looked over the cleaned area of the floor, smiled, and kept sweeping. His blue pin striped shirt, fading navy blue twill pants, and dark gray straw fedora showed signs of surviving many hours of creative work.

I made my way around him and sat on a wood stool at the counter. The inside of the shop was a continuation of the display windows. Unmatched small vintage tables crowded against an early 1900's glass front china cabinet with a 'Southern Most Point' ash tray, a pair of blue Hull vases and a few books on Florida nature on the shelves inside.

The wall to the right was covered with paintings, including Everglades landscapes and seascapes of the Florida Keys, signed 'Gordon Bachelor.' Several were of bright red poinciana trees in full bloom. The frames looked handcrafted, not factory made, which caught my eye.

Behind the counter large pieces of antique furniture were crowded against a shelving partition, open to the high ceiling, that separated the framing workshop in the back. A sign tacked to a shelf read: **"No Framing Orders! Please DO NOT insist!"**

He backed towards the door with his pile of sandy dirt and leaves growing, mumbled something to his dog, and nodded to people passing by.

"What's your dog's name?" I asked.

"Hoss."

"How did you happen to name him that?"

"Well...," he pushed back his hat thoughtfully, leaning on his broom. "His mama was a miniature terrier and his daddy was a dachshund. Hoss here was the largest of the litter and looked absolutely huge next to the others. So, we named him 'Hoss' after Hoss Cartwright on Bonanza."

He bent down and gave the dog an affectionate scratch on the head. Hoss opened his eyes briefly, then went back to his nap.

"I guess the dog jacket comes in handy when it's cool and breezy like today," I said. "What's the pocket for?"

"That's for his dog biscuits," he replied with a chuckle. "I usually keep a few in there so I won't have to run to the back room to get the box every time he comes beggin' a handout." He rested his broom against the wall, blocking the pile of debris, and walked behind the counter.

Mr. Bachelor looked to be in his forties or fifties. He had weathered suntanned skin and friendly twinkling eyes. A fringe of gray hair poked out from under his hat with specs of red paint.

"What can I do for you today?" he asked.

Having noticed his 'No Framing Orders! Please DO NOT insist!' sign, I reluctantly held up my 9" X 12" oil painting of a sailboat in blue and white. "I'd like to have this framed in something with a nautical look to it. Maybe something like that one on your painting of the lighthouse."

He shifted his body, and adjusted his fedora as he picked up my painting and looked it over. "I'm pretty busy right now!" he said with a feeling of urgency. "I'm not sure when I'd get to it."

"Oh, I see," I replied, startled by his change of demeanor. "Well, there's no rush. I really like your frames because they are so unique. "What kind of wood do you use? And, how do you make the markings on them?"

"I like pine or spruce. It's easy to get, and less expensive." Pointing to his paintings on the wall he went on, appearing to relax. "I make the grooves with an ice pick and I notch the edges with a knife. Some I stain white, or walnut, or whatever color I want. Sometimes I varnish them to get a Spanish or rustic look. The white frames I wipe down a bit to let the grain of the wood show through."

As he talked, I noticed other differences in the frames on his paintings. Some narrow, like his lighthouse painting, others were broad with a second layer of narrow wood. Shades of brown, grey or white gave them a driftwood feeling.

"Good morning, Gordon!" called a man in a white sports coat from the doorway. "How are you doing this morning?"

"Hello there, Doc." He responded, tipping his hat. "Say, I should have your picture ready later today. I've had a mess cleanin' up after all that storm last night, but I'll be sure to get it done."

"No rush," Doc reassured him. "Any news on your property?"

"We went down there over the weekend." He replied, walking towards the door. He leaned over and gave Hoss a biscuit. "No news from the bank yet. Sure does take a long time."

Doc nodded in agreement with a sympathetic smile, waved and walked back to the sidewalk.

"I'm movin' down to the Keys in another year or so," Gordon announced proudly. "Goin' to build a place with a small motel unit, a workshop for my framing business, and living area upstairs for my wife and me."

"Sounds great," I replied, noticing more things squeezed into the small space in front of the counter and on the side wall. "Where did you get all these things?"

A happy distant look came over his face as he surveyed the hodgepodge I was looking at, "Oh, I pick them up here and there."

"I get some of the things from auctions around here," he went on. "Some came from very prominent families. That picture of the boy and the goat, and the one over there of the gaucho and his horse, I bought from a wealthy South American."

"That's a 1902 barber chair from Burdine's," he motioned towards, "try it out."

I climbed into the once-plush, black leather barber chair. The soft padded arms and adjustable headrest were in good condition, considering its age. With a bit of polish, the chrome trim, foot rest and levers for reclining the chair, would shine again.

"Some things I picked up in North Carolina. That ox bow is about sixty or seventy years old, I guess. Belonged to my wife's father. My family has a cabin up there near Boone.

If ya' get away from the cities, out in the country, you run onto these little general stores. Why, you can find real old antiques out there for next to nothin'."

He turned and pointed to a long shelf on the back wall. "That's where I picked up that tobacco cutter, and that bean bin over in the corner." He picked up a vintage coffee mill from the end of the counter and set it in front of me.

"Ever see one like this? One with 'Telephone Mill' on it?" He inspected it thoroughly, as if for the first time.

"No, I don't think so," I replied, enjoying his expressions of delight when he reminisced. Everything brought back a pleasant memory, or an interesting story of where it came from, or who it belonged to.

He reminded me of my grandfather who always had wonderful stories about his life crossing Iowa in a covered wagon. I could listen to him for hours. I checked my watch to see if I had still time on my parking meter, and settled back into the barber chair.

"Were you born in North Carolina?"

"No, I was born in a little town upstate called Hampton, Florida. Just a small town not far from Gainesville. Ever hear of it?"

"Yes, I lived in Gainesville a while. Hampton is northeast of there, isn't it?" It prompted flash-backs of when I worked as a long-distance telephone operator in Gainesville and the small 'ring-down' towns like Hampton.

"Well, I'll be! It sure is!" he exclaimed with a big grin, pushing his fedora back.

"Did you move here from Hampton?" I asked, curious to know about what brought him to Miami.

"No, after the war I went to school at Grand Central School of Art in New York City. Then later, I studied some more over in New Jersey at the Newark School of Signs." He walked over to the wall and removed a small painting, typical of the early 1900's era.

"This is an original sketch of one of the murals I painted in a nightclub in Greenwich Village. I did murals all the way around the whole place. It was quite a job."

He returned the artwork to its place of honor as he continued. "It was around 1935 when I came to the Grove. I did some sign painting for a while. Also did some work for Mr. Collins over at Tropical Race Track around then. Sold a few landscape paintings on the side."

"I enjoyed fooling around with wood working, so I started making my own frames and long around 1948 I started selling them. Had a small shop over in Commodore Plaza where the bakery used to be. Then, I got where I needed more room, so I came over here."

"People come from all over to buy my frames." he said with pride, waving towards a stack of frames leaning against the wall near the door to his studio in the back. "One artist even comes down from Ft. Lauderdale and gets twenty-five or thirty at a crack. Some of the performing folks that come in to the Grove Playhouse get frames from me, too. Pat Henning, the comedian, guess he's before your time … Eddie Burke, Reginald Gardner … he's another old-timer … Ethel Merman." The expression in his eyes as he remembered another special person or another special time in his life, was captivating.

"I guess I'd better be going," I said, catching a glimpse of the time. "I have to pick my daughter up from school." I eased down from my perch in the barber chair, wondering if I was going to be looking for another framer.

He picked up my painting again, made a few notes on the back of the type of frame I wanted.

"Well, I'm awfully busy this week, but...." He took off his fedora and scratched his head. "You come back in a week. I should have this ready for you by then."

Over the years, I made sure to allow an hour or two when I went to the Grove to drop off my paintings for framing. Each visit began with Gordon's disclaimer of how busy he was, not sure of when he would have time. Then, after catching me up on his plans for moving to the Keys, I'd take my seat in the barber chair and listen about past and recent celebrity customers from the Grove Playhouse, and more about his life as a graphic artist in New York.

Maryann Higly Hamilton has a BSed-Art from FIU and a Master of Art Therapy from Vermont College. Retired from Dade & Pinellas public schools, she is a published author, and in her leisure time you may find her traveling, creating art, writing children's books, or with her daughter at a Kentucky horse show.

DWG

ALEX PAULSON and JENNIFER SHOVAN

Solar: Guardian of The Nexus

Chapter One

A voice whispered: "My Guardian." It sounded like the voice of a woman, but it was so faint I could hardly hear it. I tried to determine where it came from, but I was surrounded by nothing but a dark space full of stars. That was when I saw it – the blinding flash of light illuminating the darkness. It took the form of a griffin made of hard light and flapping its majestic wings. It stared sternly at my eyes and moved closer to me. I flinched and ended up falling on my butt. As soon as it landed with a powerful yet graceful impact, it gave a softer facial expression.

"Do not be afraid," it said. "I have no intention of harming you."

Still a nervous wreck, I could barely ask, "Who ... Who are you?"

"I am Serina," she answered. "I'm honored to finally make your acquaintance, Cea'Var Jah-Nar of Spektarum."

Now that she seemed to be less intimidating, I stood up and approached her. My fear was repressed, at least temporarily, but now I grew curious.

"Cea'Var Jah-Nar?" I asked. "My name is Carter Johnson, and I'm from Planet Earth."

Serina tried to suppress a laugh. "But of course, Carter. You were raised on the planet Earth and were given a human name, but your origins lie beyond these stars." She spread her wings out and pointed toward the heavens. I looked at the stars, a beautiful sight. But Serina's claim was outlandish.

"I don't understand," I said.

"You will. I know this is all very confusing for you, but now that your chains are broken, the time has come to meet your destiny."

Even more confused, and I grew frustrated. "Look, bird-lady, I don't know what you're talking about as far as chains being broken, or meeting a destiny. I'm just a sixteen-year-old kid who goes to school and lives with his grandfather and best friend/god-brother. I'm not special!"

Serina kept her calm and soft expression. "That's where you're wrong, young one. But there is no more time for our conversation."

The space began to shake. I almost fell again but managed to regain my balance. Serina lifted her wings and flew straight up into the darkness. Her surrounding light died.

"Wait!" I yelled. "I still have more questions!"

The shaking grew worse. Stars were falling, and what might've been considered the ground began breaking apart. I ran as fast as I could from the "earthquake" if you could call it that, but it caught up with me, and I fell, screaming into infinite darkness. No stars, no talking bird lady, just pure darkness and the sound of my screaming, echoing voice.

That's when I woke up in my bed. I was saturated with sweat, my hair all in my face, soaked as well. Grabbing my torso and my sweaty face, I laughed.

"I'm alive," I shouted

It had all been a dream, a completely crazy dream. Then came a knock on the door and a man saying, "Carter, get up! You and Victor will be late for school!"

"Uh, coming, Grandpa!"

I threw my blanket across my bed, racing to grab my clothes. It took a few minutes to get dressed. I wasn't trying to look like a model or anything, but I didn't want to look like a homeless kid either. Kids at school make fun of me enough as it is; I don't need them calling me a trash panda or something like that. I pulled on blue jeans, a red t-shirt, and a brown flight jacket for the early fall chill. I brushed my hair, but since not to be late for school, I didn't do a good job at it either. Not that my hair was usually that great looking anyway.

Before I shot out the bedroom for breakfast, I grabbed a sun necklace from my dresser. Go ahead and laugh— "You wear a necklace? That's so lame." Whatever, it's the only connection I have to my parents. More specifically, my mom. My grandpa said she gave it to me before she died when I was a baby. It was a way for me to know that even though she may be gone, she'll never leave my heart. The same went for my dad too, but I know even less about him.

Grandpa could not talk about him without getting upset. I pressed the necklace to my lips, kissed it, and held it close to my heart. I then put it on under my shirt. I opened the door, raced down the stairs, and slid my way onto the slippery kitchen floor, crashing into the chair and nutting myself. I fell and groaned in pain, holding my groin.

My brother Victor, drinking his coffee, looking at his phone, and not helping, then said dryly, "Nice entrance."

I stopped groaning, tried to get up, and managed to say, "Aren't you going to help, smartass?"

Victor just stared at his phone and sipped his coffee. It was like he was ignoring the fact that I existed. After a while, I grabbed the chair and sat at the table without collapsing back down like a potato sack.

It appeared Grandpa made his famous burnt, thin pancakes, again. I took a bit and spit it out. "How on earth does someone freaking screw up pancakes?"

"How do you end up sliding on the floor and nutting yourself with the chair? "Victor retorted.

"Very funny. What are you still doing here anyway? Normally you'd be long since gone and waiting in the cafeteria. Especially with your new 'extracurricular' activity at night."

Victor put down his phone and leaned back on the chair. "Quiet night," he answered. "How have you been? You've been having a lot of strange dreams and nightmares since I've been back, and after being kidnapped by Project Ragnarok."

I shrugged, chuckled. "They're just dreams, Vic. That's all."

Victor then leaned to put the chair back in place and crossed his hands together. "Are you sure about that? Dreams have a powerful effect on our everyday lives. They can affect our emotions, relationships with other people—"

"I get it! This is also coming from a guy who thinks it's a good idea to cut everyone out of his life for eight years and dress up like Batman every night for the past two months!"

Victor shook his head. "Batman?"

I raised my arms again. "What? You have!"

"Enough!" came a stern voice from the kitchen. An elderly man with silver silky long hair, a nice suit, eyes as yellow as mine, and a walking cane approached us, annoyed. Victor went back to drinking his coffee, and I tried shoving as many burnt pancakes down my throat as I possibly could. His face lit up when he saw Victor.

"Ah, Victor. How kind of you to be able to join us for breakfast this morning."

Victor closed his eyes again. "Morning, Professor. The night was quiet."

Then Grandpa turned to me with his disapproving expression again.

After I managed to swallow the last burnt pancake, I put down my fork and said, "Uh, morning, Grandpa."

He shook his head, sighed. "Carter, how many times must I tell you to quit harassing Victor? Not to mention, look at yourself." He pointed his cane at me. "Do you honestly expect to be taken seriously with your face covered in pancake particles and syrup?"

"Sorry, Grandpa, just had a rough night, and I was hungry." I turned around and looked at Victor. "And sorry for giving you such a hard time, Vic."

Victor scoffed. "I know you didn't mean it, Carter. Just want to make sure you're alright. I may not always show it, but we're brothers till the end."

Victor gave out his hand. I shook. "Brothers till the end." He smiled, which is rare because he doesn't smile unless he's in "Rich-Kid" mode. When we let go, we realized I had forgotten to wash my hands. Fortunately, he was wearing leather gloves, but he still had a disgusted look at the syrup on them. Victor took off his gloves and got up from his chair to grab a new pair. I ran to the bathroom to wash my hands.

"Those boys," Grandpa chuckled.

Victor and I raced outside to pick up our friend Joey next door. I knocked and a dark-skinned woman wearing a sea-green robe, flip-flops, and a completely frizzled afro opened the door. She looked like she needed some coffee, but neither of us said anything about that.

"Hi, Doctor Marks. Is Joey ready?" I asked.

She rubbed her eyes and took a better look at Victor and me, then grinned. "Oh hello, boys. Sorry, just a long shift at the hospital." She turned around and shouted "Joseph! Carter and Victor are here to take you to school!" We heard someone rustling around upstairs, surely Joey. He spent every second he could behind his computer, whether it was homework, one of his computer projects, or playing *Tech: The Assembly*. It was a wonder that he was not blind nor gained any weight considering he ate mostly junk food.

Doctor Marks sighed. "I'm so sorry boys. He's probably playing that silly game of his again."

Victor put his hands in his pockets. "Do you just want us to go on ahead, Doctor? —Ow!" he cried when I elbowed him.

"Victor," I said, irritated that he would suggest our going ahead.

"What?" he asked. "This is the fourth time this week. And last time we were ten minutes late." We glared at each other. Even though Victor was secretly a vigilante that terrorized even the most hardcore psychopaths, he never had luck intimidating me.

"Boys," Doctor Marks interrupted on our intense staring contest. "Ain't got time for this foolishness."

Victor and I broke our staring contest and said, "Sorry, Doctor Marks."

"I will get Joey. I didn't know this was going on, so I'll be right back."

She gently closed the door. We waited for a couple of minutes. I paced around the porch while Victor kept still with his hands in his pocket and his eyes closed.

"Will you stop pacing?" he asked. "It's making me edgy."

"What's taking them so long?"

We heard arguing from inside. It seemed like Doctor Marks was chewing Joey out for spending too much time on his computer. I tried to look through the window shutters, but they were closed tight.

Victor rolled his eyes. "You know it's rude to look through someone's window."

"Shut up. You break into people's houses. That's both rude and illegal."

Finally, Joey thrust the door open while Doctor Marks was still chewing him out. "Your life is school and home. And no computer unless it's for school purposes for three weeks. Or if you need to contact me or your father."

Joey stomped his right foot, threw his back at me, and shouted, "Alright! I get it, Mama! This time I wasn't even playing the f-ing game!"

Ducking to avoid being hit by Joey's heavy backpack, Victor and I took a few steps back away from him. If there was one thing his mom could not stand, it was cursing. She grabbed Joey's wrist.

"Lil' boy, you use that nasty language again, so help me God, I'll whip your behind in front of your friends at school, understand?" She gave a deadly serious glance. Part of me was surprised she didn't do it now since Victor and I were some of the few real friends Joey had.

"Yes ma'am," he said timidly.

She let go, and Joey ran straight for Victor's car. Doctor Marks still glared at him like she was going to spank him, but then she took a deep breath and looked at us.

"I'm so sorry you two had to see that."

"It's Ok, Doctor M," I said. "It's not like we haven't seen it before."

"I know, but still. You two have better things to be doing. I appreciate you coming down and taking Joey to school since I and Andre are usually at work. Especially after Alfonso's..." Her voice cracked for a moment, and then she went silent.

Alfonso was Joey's older brother who followed in their dad's footsteps working in the police department.

"We'll make sure to keep Joey out of trouble, Doctor," Victor said, approaching Doctor Marks and placing his right hand on her shoulder. She took Victor's hand and held it gently while patting it.

"Thank you. Both of you. Now go on. You three need to get your education for the day."

I said, "Will do, Doc."

Victor nodded, and Doctor Marks let go of his hand. All three of us left the porch and got into Victor's car.

The ride to school was mostly quiet. Joey normally played on his computer in the back seat, but considering what went down with his mom, he decided against it. Instead, he was zipping his Miles Morales Spider-Man jacket up and down. I looked out the window, seeing the pretty suburban view rush along. Victor focused on his driving, and he's usually quiet anyway.

"You know you could go a little easier on your mom, dude," I said, instantly regretting it.

Joey scowled at me. "Sorry. Didn't know you were an expert on moms, considering you don't have one."

"Hey!" I said. "Not cool man. I'm just saying, you have been an ass to her for the past two months. You're more focused on that computer than usual, looking into your dad's police records and reports, and hunting down a shadow that might not even exist."

"Nightwatcher is real, Carter! You even said it yourself when he rescued you."

"I don't know what I saw," I denied. "It could've just been a cop that got lucky and found me in that creepy and dingy lab. I was so out of it. It could've been Barny the Purple Dinosaur."

I knew it was Victor that found me, but it's not like I could tell Joey. Keeping Victor's double identity was crucial to his operations as Nightwatcher, plus Joey's already been through enough with Alf's death. His reaction to telling him Victor is Nightwatcher could go either way in whether he'd be relived or infuriated. Lastly, it's not my secret to tell. The only reason I know is that I know Victor better than anyone. He never got over what happened to his dad, and chances are he's never going to. Nightwatcher is just his way of dealing with it. Most people would see it as an excuse to get revenge, but in reality, it's his penance.

"Knock it off," Victor ordered.

Joey grew even more irritated. "Come on Vic. Back me up. Ever since you got back, strange things have been going on around town. Between your ma, Nightwatcher, and now there are rumors that aliens and warrior princesses are here."

Victor chuckled. "Aliens, and warrior princesses? I think you've been spending too much time on your laptop Joey. Or in comics, I'm not sure which."

"I'm not lying!" Joey slammed his fist on his left knee. "There have been pictures of a giant lizard creature, with a giant sword, cape, and war helmet. Everything. And there are blurry pictures of some kind of girl dressed like a warrior princess who can command animals and has a saber sword."

I finally started chuckling. "Come on Joey. The girl, maybe she's some kind of a cosplayer. But there's no such thing as aliens or superheroes. Nightwatcher just sounds like a nut who finally had it with the supposed 'goody-two shoe' lawmen. But come on, aliens?"

"I know what I saw!"

"Yeah," I scoffed "On those crazy conspiracy theory websites or rumors from the precinct. Besides, why would aliens want to come here? The only thing they'll catch is human idiocy, and no one wants that."

Just then a huge bump hit the back of the car. Joey nearly shot out of his seat, despite having his seatbelt on. It didn't affect me that much, other than I hit my head on the roof of the car. Victor almost hit his face on the driving wheel. While rubbing my head, I turned back to look at Joey.

"You okay?"

"Yeah, I'm fine."

I sighed in relief and looked at Victor. "What the hell was that?".

Victor adjusted the rearview mirror and cursed. "It's Duncan."

"What?" I turned to look outside, seeing Duncan driving his blue Mustang with his ugly-faced friends. They were hooting like owls when they weren't laughing, and they all kept flipping us off.

"That idiot has finally lost his mind," I shouted. "Is he trying to kill us?"

Victor turned in my direction. "What do you think?"

 A sophomore psychology major at Purdue Global University, Alexander Paulson is co-creator of the Nexus Universe. This is his first time sharing a piece of his writing, and has been mentored by the group. He has joined us from Indiana via our online meetings.

 A Florida native and avid reader from the age of 3, Jennifer Shovan is a lover of sci-fi/fantasy. She lives at home with her parents, younger sister, and a very noisy Sheltie. She is a proponent of civil rights, particularly for LGBTQ+ youth, and a prolific creator of characters.

DWG

IN CLOSING

The year 2021 has been one for the history books. At first, when the nation thought we had defeated the covid virus, we at DWG believed we could soon renew our in-person group meetings at the Dunedin Public Library, but then with the variant virus, we realized our isolation must continue. Then, with the magic of the Internet we stayed connected each Friday morning and continued supporting each other's literary efforts. The duress transformed us from a group to a family. This anthology embodies the work that went on despite our circumstances and our often-low spirits. The anthology enlivened the agony and ecstasy of our creative processes.

No matter his or her writing level, every participant of DWG was encouraged to enter a piece to the anthology. Each piece had to pass a rigorous proofing and editing process, and in this volume, we have presented our labors with pride and pleasure. We welcome you, our readers, to respond with an Amazon review, and we thank our local vendors for making our work available here in the Tampa Bay Area.

In this year, characterized by national division and ongoing pandemic tragedy, members of Dunedin Writers Group bonded around our art to express and to share our various truths. In spite of the turmoil, we found friendship and support, and we look forward to better times for our nation. In the meantime, we will get back to our keyboards and prepare for next year's anthology. We hope this year's edition has brought pleasure, maybe even solace, to you, our cherished readers. If you enjoyed this edition, check out our previous two, available from any of our members, on Amazon, and in the Dunedin library.

So, because we started with a poem from acclaimed early 20th Century poet William Carlos Williams, let us close with another, this one about the creative process—

> I wanted to write a poem
> that you would understand.
> For what good is it to me
> if you don't understand it?
> But you got to try hard –
> But –
> Well, you know how
> the young girls run giggling
> on Park Avenue after dark
> when they ought to be home in bed?
> Well,
> that's the way it is with me somehow.

From "January Morning"
Selected Poems, 1917

Jon Michael Miller, Editor

DWG

Made in the USA
Columbia, SC
02 November 2021